Less Web Development Essentials

Use CSS preprocessing to streamline the development and maintenance of your web applications

Bass Jobsen

BIRMINGHAM - MUMBAI

Less Web Development Essentials

First published: April 2014

Production Reference: 1170414

Published by Packt Publishing Ltd.
Livery Place
35 Livery Street
Birmingham B3 2PB, UK.

ISBN 978-1-78398-146-5

www.packtpub.com

Cover Image by Faiz J. Fattohi (faizfattohi@gmail.com)

Credits

Author
Bass Jobsen

Reviewers
Marcus Bointon

Simone Deponti

Austin Pickett

Commissioning Editor
Ashwin Nair

Acquisition Editor
Richard Harvey

Content Development Editor
Sruthi Kutty

Technical Editors
Kapil Hemnani

Faisal Siddiqui

Project Coordinator
Sageer Parkar

Proofreaders
Maria Gould

Paul Hindle

Indexer
Tejal Soni

Graphics
Ronak Dhruv

Production Coordinator
Arvindkumar Gupta

Cover Work
Arvindkumar Gupta

Copy Editor
Karuna Narayanan

Foreword

Before you dive into this book, let me give you a little bit of background. In the summer of 2009, I was writing CSS for a project of mine and had developed a habit of questioning every piece of technology I used. I enjoyed CSS for the most part, but one thing bothered me: I couldn't experiment like I wanted to. I was designing a lot back then, and I strongly believed in designing directly in the browser. This meant being able to change the overall tone and style of the page quickly to try different ideas. With the usual way of organizing CSS, this can be difficult. You have to keep classes small and "composable", shifting the burden to the HTML. CSS is great when you need to translate an existing, final design to the Web. However, that's not how things work very often. More and more designers are jumping straight into CSS, closing the gap between design and implementation, and they need a tool that they can use all the way through, from ideation to finished product.

I started thinking of workarounds such as separating colors from other properties so that all classes that were of the same color would be defined together. However, I wanted colors to depend on other colors; I wanted to describe the theme as "relationships" between colors, not static values. I wanted to turn a knob and have the page change from one look to another. This was plainly impossible with the CSS of 2009. I looked for solutions in the form of preprocessors and found a few, but most of them were doing too much; they were fixing things that weren't broken, such as the core syntax of the language that I happened to like.

So, I decided to put something together that would do what I wanted; the first version of Less was born. It was quickly apparent that I wasn't the only one looking for something like this. The idea was simple, but it was a step in the right direction.

Five years later, looking back at this is interesting. If I had run into these problems with the experience I have today, would I have followed the same path? I think my intuition was correct, but never could I have predicted how difficult it is to get something like this right. It's one thing to design something for yourself; it's a completely different thing when it has to work for everyone. This has made me appreciate the quality of the work that went into the CSS specification all the more, as well as the working group's cautiousness in moving forward.

It's important to remember that Less is an extension of CSS, and much of the power of Less comes from its support for plain CSS. It's easy to forget when you have access to all the extra capabilities. However, those who know when and how to use both technologies will enjoy the greatest flexibility and control over their creations.

Alexis Sellier
@cloudhead
Creator of Less

About the Author

Bass Jobsen has been programming for the Web since 1995, from C to PHP, always looking for the most accessible interfaces. He has a special interest in the process between a designer and programmer. He believes that interfaces should work independent of a device or browser. For these reasons, working with grids and meta languages in designs makes him happy. He always looks forward to new opportunities in the Semantic and Responsive Web.

He uses Less in his daily job for web design tasks and WordPress theme development as well as other Twitter Bootstrap apps.

He is always happy to help you. He can be reached at `http://stackoverflow.com/users/1596547/bass-jobsen`.

Currently, he writes a blog (`http://bassjobsen.weblogs.fm/`), programs LBS for mobile devices (`http://www.gizzing.nl`), makes cool websites (such as `http://www.streetart.nl/`), and counsels Jamedo Websites (`http://www.jamedowebsite.nl/`) in setting up the technical environment and requirements for their business.

You can also check out his Bootstrap WordPress Starters Theme (JBST) and other projects at GitHub at `https://github.com/bassjobsen`.

> *"I choose a lazy person to do a hard job. Because a lazy person will find an easy way to do it."*

> – Bill Gates

Acknowledgments

This book is for Colinda, Kiki, Dries, Wolf, and Leny.

Recently, I reviewed *Getting Started with Zurb Foundation 4* by Andrew D. Patterson and *Learning Zurb Foundation* by Kevin Horek. After finishing this book, I will start writing *Less Web Development Cookbook* for Packt Publishing.

Although I have written many blogs and technical project requirements in the past years, this is the first book I have written to be published. Writing this book wasn't possible without the support of my family, Caroliene, and the people of Vivent. Richard Harvey was a patient and excellent motivator and critical reader. Sruthi Kutty helped me dot the i's and cross the t's. Finally, I will thank the reviewers of this book, Simone Deponti, Austin Pickett, and Marcus Bointon, for their critical and valuable suggestions, which make this book even better.

About the Reviewers

Marcus Bointon has been a Less committer for the last couple of years, having developed a taste for Less during the early versions of Twitter Bootstrap. He has a Bachelor's degree in Computer Science from the University of London and a Master's degree from Loughborough University of Technology. He's been involved in computing since 1981 and developing for the Web since 1993. He has extensive experience in many development languages (mainly PHP), Linux and OpenBSD server admin, MySQL database design and admin, e-mail infrastructure, network design, and much more. He is the maintainer of the very popular PHPMailer e-mail sending library.

Marcus is the co-founder and technical director of Synchromedia Limited, a UK-based company behind the smartmessages.net e-mail marketing service, and a UK partner for the 1CRM open source CRM system.

He lives with his wife and two kids in the French Alps, where he can indulge his passion for skiing and mountain biking.

Simone Deponti is a web developer from Milan, Italy. He has eight years of experience in the field, primarily in CMSes, and has contributed to some open source projects, most notably the Plone CMS. He is also the author of a small debugging tool for Less and FireLess, and he wrote the initial debugging support in the Less compiler.

He works for Abstract, a web technology agency based in Italy and Germany, as a developer and project manager. You can find him at events around the world, focusing on Python, JavaScript, and CMSes.

Austin Pickett is a freelance web developer based out of Boston, MA. He has been interested in programming since he was a child and is never seen without a computer nearby. As a self-taught designer and developer, he has worked with several of his own clients to turn their websites or applications into a reality.

Austin has his own freelance career in which he works closely with clients to create their applications. He has worked with a wide array of clients from The National Academy of Best-selling Authors and vacation property owners to web design firms.

Thanks go out to my father, Shawn Pickett, for without him I would have never been interested in computers, and to my best friend and rival, Talasan Nicholson, for without him I would have no local competition or a buddy to ping at 2 AM.

www.PacktPub.com

Support files, eBooks, discount offers and more

You might want to visit www.PacktPub.com for support files and downloads related to your book.

Did you know that Packt offers eBook versions of every book published, with PDF and ePub files available? You can upgrade to the eBook version at www.PacktPub.com and as a print book customer, you are entitled to a discount on the eBook copy. Get in touch with us at service@packtpub.com for more details.

At www.PacktPub.com, you can also read a collection of free technical articles, sign up for a range of free newsletters and receive exclusive discounts and offers on Packt books and eBooks.

http://PacktLib.PacktPub.com

Do you need instant solutions to your IT questions? PacktLib is Packt's online digital book library. Here, you can access, read and search across Packt's entire library of books.

Why Subscribe?
- Fully searchable across every book published by Packt
- Copy and paste, print and bookmark content
- On demand and accessible via web browser

Free Access for Packt account holders

If you have an account with Packt at www.PacktPub.com, you can use this to access PacktLib today and view nine entirely free books. Simply use your login credentials for immediate access.

Table of Contents

Preface

After the introduction of HTML 4.01 in 1999, the Web changed fast. Many new devices such as tablets and mobile phones saw the light of day. Mobile Internet became faster, cheaper, and more stable. The W3C started the HTML5 working group in 2007. In December 2012, W3C designated HTML5 as a candidate recommendation. HTML5 works with CSS3. Today, all major browsers (Chrome, Safari, Firefox, Opera, IE) offer HTML5 support.

The impact of CSS3 has been huge. Nowadays, CSS3 is not only used to style your HTML documents, but CSS3 also plays an important role in the responsibility of your designs. Last but not least, CSS3 extends CSS with features such as animations and transitions.

We don't need external flash components for complex animation. Take a look at `http://www.hongkiat.com/blog/css3-animation-transition-demos/` or look at the funny owl in the following screenshot:

The owl in the preceding screenshot has been built with HTML5 and CSS3 alone. The live version can wink and look by pressing the buttons.

Responsive designs allow you to build one version of your website with only one code base which functions well and looks good on different devices such as mobile phones, tablets, and desktops. There won't be any technical reason to build different mobile and desktop versions, as shown in the following screenshot:

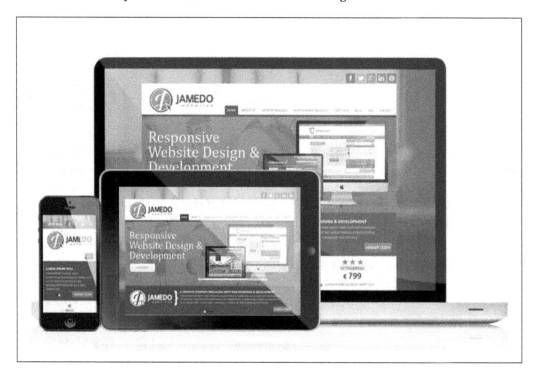

With all this new stuff, the work of the CSS (or web) developer becomes more complex. A web developer needs to know about complex CSS3, the difference between browsers and devices, animations, and other style effects. Writing correct and functional CSS code will be the first thing; keeping this code readable, maintainable, and working on all major browsers will be the second thing. CSS files grow and become untidy in the development and maintenance processes. CSS doesn't have the ability to modify the existing values or reuse common styles. Also, doing math or defining variables is not possible in CSS. This is where Less comes into the frame.

Less (Leaner CSS) is a dynamic stylesheet language designed by Alexis Sellier. Started in 2010, it is now maintained and extended by the Less core team. Less helps you make your CSS code maintainable, reusable, and prevent code duplications.

In this book, you will learn how to write, compile, and understand Less. We will help you do faster and more cost-effective web development. You will get practical tips to integrate Less in your current and new projects. After reading this book, you will write clear and readable CSS3 with Less. Instead of spending your time on debugging your complex CSS code for a specific device or browser, you can pay more attention to your real design tasks.

Your clients will be happy with your advanced and stable designs. This will reduce the development and maintenance time and hence the cost of designing.

Less extends CSS with functions and variables. In a semantic sense, valid CSS is also valid Less. The initial versions of Less were written in Ruby; now, Less is written in JavaScript.

Less is called a CSS precompiler. This means that the end product will be used for production. The end product in this case will be valid, compact, and readable CSS code. Besides, the precompiling Less code can also compile in real time. Less offers server-side and client-side options to do this. Real-time client-side compilation via LESS.js in a modern web browser makes testing easy. Server-side compilations offer opportunities to build applications with Less as well as create dynamic CSS.

Also, others know the power of Less. Projects such as Twitter's Bootstrap and Roots, a WordPress starter theme, both rely on Less. These projects build clear and extendable frameworks with Less. You can't ignore this proof. Stop writing cumbersome CSS with bugs and browser defects and learn about Less by reading this book.

Less is open source and licensed under the Apache license. At the time of writing this book, the latest version is 1.7. The source code of Less will be maintained on GitHub. Everybody will be allowed to contribute to it. You can use Less free of charge.

What this book covers

Chapter 1, *Improving Web Development with Less*, shows how CSS3 brought advanced functions such as gradients, transitions, and animations to web designers. It also explains how, on the other hand, CSS code became more complex and difficult to maintain. Less helps you make your CSS maintainable, reusable, and prevent code duplications.

Chapter 2, *Using Variables and Mixins*, explains why variables allow you to specify widely-used values in a single place and then reuse them throughout the style sheet, thus making global changes as easy as changing one line of code. Mixins allow you to embed all the properties of a class into another class by simply including the class name as one of its properties. The chapter also explains what parametric mixins are and how to use them.

Chapter 3, *Nested Rules, Operations, and Built-in Functions*, explains the use of nested rules for making inheritance clear and for making shorter style sheets. The chapter also explains how to create complex relationships between properties and how to use the built-in functions of Less.

Chapter 4, *Avoid Reinventing the Wheel*, teaches you how Less code and mixins can become complex because they handle different browsers and devices. The chapter also explains prebuilt mixins and other sources that help you (re)use them.

Chapter 5, *Integrate Less in Your Own Projects*, teaches you how to organize your files for new projects or get the projects you maintain ready for using Less.

Chapter 6, *Bootstrap 3, WordPress, and Other Applications*, explains what Bootstrap is and shows the strength of using Less with Bootstrap. The chapter also teaches you how to build web applications with Less or integrate it in your WordPress themes.

What you need for this book

To understand and get the full benefit of the contents of this book, we expect you to have built a website with CSS previously. A basic understanding of CSS will be required. Understanding CSS selectors and CSS precedence will help you get the most out of this book. We will introduce these CSS aspects briefly in the first chapter as well. Understanding the basics of using functions and parameters in functional languages such as JavaScript will be valuable, but it is not required. Don't panic if you know nothing about functions and parameters. This book contains clear examples. Even without any (functional) programming knowledge you can learn how to use Less, and this book will help you do this. The most important skill will be the willingness to learn.

All chapters of this book contain examples and example code. Running and testing these examples will help you develop your Less skills. You will need a modern web browser such as Google Chrome or Mozilla Firefox to run these examples. Use any preferred text or CSS editor to write your Less code.

Who this book is for

Every web designer who works with CSS and who wants to spend more time on real designing tasks should read this book. It doesn't matter if you are a beginner web designer or have used CSS for years; both will profit from reading this book and will learn how to utilize Less. We also recommend this book for teachers and students in modern web design and computer science. Less does not depend on a platform, language, or CMS. If you use CSS, you can and will benefit from Less.

Conventions

In this book, you will find a number of styles of text that distinguish between different kinds of information. Here are some examples of these styles, and an explanation of their meaning.

Code words in text, database table names, folder names, filenames, file extensions, pathnames, dummy URLs, and user input are shown as follows: "Note that in this case, an ID is a unique selector starting with #; the selector [id=] for the same HTML element counts as an attribute."

A block of code is set as follows:

```
.box-shadow(@style, @c) when (iscolor(@c)) {
  -webkit-box-shadow: @style @c;
  -moz-box-shadow:    @style @c;
  box-shadow:         @style @c;
}
.box-shadow(@style, @alpha: 50%) when (isnumber(@alpha)) {
  .box-shadow(@style, rgba(0, 0, 0, @alpha));
}
```

When we wish to draw your attention to a particular part of a code block, the relevant lines or items are set in bold:

```
.box-shadow(@style, @c) when (iscolor(@c)) {
  -webkit-box-shadow: @style @c;
  -moz-box-shadow:    @style @c;
  box-shadow:         @style @c;
}
.box-shadow(@style, @alpha: 50%) when (isnumber(@alpha)) {
  .box-shadow(@style, rgba(0, 0, 0, @alpha));
}
```

Any command-line input or output is written as follows:

```
# lessc -c styles.less > styles.css
```

New terms and **important words** are shown in bold. Words that you see on the screen, in menus or dialog boxes for example, appear in the text like this: "Clicking on the **Next** button moves you to the next screen."

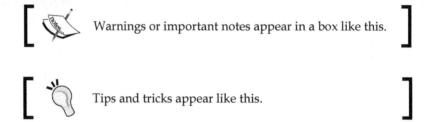

Warnings or important notes appear in a box like this.

Tips and tricks appear like this.

Reader feedback

Feedback from our readers is always welcome. Let us know what you think about this book—what you liked or may have disliked. Reader feedback is important for us to develop titles that you really get the most out of.

To send us general feedback, simply send an e-mail to feedback@packtpub.com, and mention the book title through the subject of your message.

If there is a topic that you have expertise in and you are interested in either writing or contributing to a book, see our author guide on www.packtpub.com/authors.

Customer support

Now that you are the proud owner of a Packt book, we have a number of things to help you to get the most from your purchase.

Downloading the example code

You can download the example code files for all Packt books you have purchased from your account at http://www.packtpub.com/. If you purchased this book elsewhere, you can visit http://www.packtpub.com/support/ and register to have the files e-mailed directly to you.

Errata

Although we have taken every care to ensure the accuracy of our content, mistakes do happen. If you find a mistake in one of our books—maybe a mistake in the text or the code—we would be grateful if you would report this to us. By doing so, you can save other readers from frustration and help us improve subsequent versions of this book. If you find any errata, please report them by visiting http://www.packtpub.com/support, selecting your book, clicking on the **errata submission form** link, and entering the details of your errata. Once your errata are verified, your submission will be accepted and the errata will be uploaded to our website, or added to any list of existing errata, under the Errata section of that title.

Piracy

Piracy of copyright material on the Internet is an ongoing problem across all media. At Packt, we take the protection of our copyright and licenses very seriously. If you come across any illegal copies of our works, in any form, on the Internet, please provide us with the location address or website name immediately so that we can pursue a remedy.

Please contact us at copyright@packtpub.com with a link to the suspected pirated material.

We appreciate your help in protecting our authors, and our ability to bring you valuable content.

Questions

You can contact us at questions@packtpub.com if you are having a problem with any aspect of the book, and we will do our best to address it.

1
Improving Web Development with Less

It is impossible to imagine modern web design without CSS. With CSS3, web designers are able to rely on advanced functions such as gradients, transitions, and animations. On the other hand, CSS code becomes more complex and difficult to maintain. *Less* is a CSS preprocessor that extends CSS with modern programming-language concepts. Less enables you to use variables, functions, operations, and even rule or selector nesting while coding your CSS. *Less* helps you write CSS with the **Don't Repeat Yourself (DRY)** principle. The DRY principle prevents you from repeating any kind of information in your code.

This chapter will cover the following topics:

- Introduction to CSS3
- Compiling Less into CSS
- Vendor-specific rules
- CSS3 rounded corners, animations, and gradients
- Using box-sizing border-box
- Server-side compiling and using GUI

Using CSS3 for styling your HTML

In web design, you will use HTML to describe the structure of your documents and CSS language to describe their presentation, including fonts, colors, and layout. The current standard HTML5 and CSS3 versions work on most modern browsers and mobile devices. CSS3 extends the old CSS with other new selectors, text effects, background gradients, and animations. The power of CSS3, the new functionalities, and high acceptance on mobile devices using HTML5 and CSS3 make them the standard for modern web design. The combination of HTML5 and CSS3 is ideal for building responsive websites because of their high acceptance on mobile phones (and other devices).

Together, HTML5 and CSS3 introduce many new features. You will be shown the ones that are the most significant when learning about their concepts within this book.

Using CSS Selectors to style your HTML

With *Less* (and CSS), you can style your HTML code using **selectors**. CSS selectors are patterns or names that identify which HTML elements of the web page should be styled. CSS selectors play an important role in writing *Less* code.

For `body p.article {color:red}`, the selector here is `body p.article`. Selectors don't refer exclusively to one element. They can point to more than one element and different ones can refer to the same element. For instance, a single `p` selector refers to all the `p-elements`, including the `p-elements` with a `.article` class. In the case of conflicts, **cascade** and **specificity** determine which styles should be applied. When writing *Less* code, we should keep the aforementioned rules in mind. *Less* makes it easier to write complex CSS without changing how your website looks. It doesn't introduce any limitations on your final CSS. With *Less*, you can edit well-structured code instead of changing the effect of the final CSS.

CSS3 introduces many new and handy selectors. One of them is `:nth-child(n)`, which makes it possible to style, for example, every fourth paragraph's `p` tag in an HTML document. Such selectors add powerful functions to CSS3. Now we are able to perform operations with CSS alone, whereas, in the past we needed JavaScript or hardcoded styles (or classes at the very least). Again, this is one of the reasons to learn *Less*. Powerful selectors will make CSS more important, but CSS code also becomes cumbersome and difficult to maintain. *Less* will prevent this problem in CSS, even making complex code flexible and easy to maintain.

 Please visit `https://developer.mozilla.org/en-US/docs/Web/CSS/Reference#Selectors` for a complete list of CSS selectors.

Specificity, Inheritance, and Cascade in CSS

In most cases, many CSS styles can be applied on the same HTML element, but only one of them will win. *W3C specifications* describe the rules for which CSS styles get the most precedence and will ultimately be applied. You can find these specifications in the following section.

The rules regarding the order of importance have not significantly changed with CSS3. They are briefly mentioned to help you understand some of the common pitfalls with *Less/CSS* and how to solve them. Sooner or later, you will be in a situation where you're trying to apply a CSS style to an element, but its effect stays invisible. You will reload, pull out your hair, and check for typos again and again, but nothing will help. This is because in most of these cases, your style will be overruled with another style that has a higher precedence.

The global rules for Cascade in CSS are as follows:

- Find all the CSS declarations that apply to the element and property in question.
- **Inline styles** have the highest precedence, except for `!important`. The `!important` statement in CSS is a keyword used to add weight to a declaration. The `!important` statement is added at the end of a CSS property value. After this, check who set the declaration; styles set by the author get a higher precedence than the styles defined by the user or browser (default). Default means the styles are set by the web browser, author styles are defined by CSS in the web page, and user styles are set by the user via the settings of his or her web browser. The importance of the user is higher than the default, and the code with the `!important` statement (see *Chapter 2, Using Variables and Mixins* for its meaning in *Less*) will always get the highest precedence. Note that browsers such as Firefox have options to disable pages in order to use other alternatives to user-defined fonts. Here, the user settings overrule the CSS of the web page. This way of overruling the page settings is not part of the CSS precedence unless they are set using `!important`.
- Calculate the specificity, which is discussed in the following section.
- If two or more rules have the same precedence and specificity, the one declared last wins.

As a *Less/CSS* designer, you will be making use of the calculated CSS specificity in most cases.

How CSS specificity works

Every CSS declaration gets a specificity, which will be calculated from the type of declaration and the selectors used in its declaration. Inline styles will always get the highest specificity and will always be applied (unless overwritten by the first two Cascade rules). In practice, you should not use inline styles in many cases as it will break the DRY principle. It will also disable you from changing your styles on a centralized location only and will prevent you from using *Less* for styling.

An example of an inline style declaration is shown as follows:

```
<p style="color:#0000ff;">
```

After this, the number of IDs in the selector will be the next indicator to calculate specificity. The `#footer #leftcolumn {}` selector has 2 IDs, the `#footer {}` selector has 1 ID, and so on.

> Note that in this case, an ID is a unique selector starting with #; the selector `[id=]` for the same HTML element counts as an **attribute**. This means that `div.#unique {}` has 1 ID and `div[id="unique"] {}` has 0 IDs and 1 attribute.

If the number of IDs for two declarations is equal, the number of **classes**, **pseudo classes**, and **attributes** of the selector will be of importance. Classes start with a dot. For example, `.row` is a class. Pseudo classes, such as `:hover` and `:after`, start with a colon, and attributes, of course, are `href`, `alt`, `id`, and so on.

The `#footer a.alert:hover {}` selector scores 2 (1 class and 1 pseudo class) and the `#footer div.right a.alert:hover {}` selector scores 3 (2 classes and 1 pseudo class).

If this value is equal for both declarations, we can start counting the **elements** and **pseudo elements**. The latest variable will be defined with a double colon (`::`). Pseudo elements allow authors to refer to otherwise inaccessible information, such as `::first-letter`. The following example shows you how that works.

The `#footer div a{}` selector scores 2 (2 elements) and the `#footer div p a {}` selector scores 3 (3 elements).

You should now know what to do when your style isn't directly applied. In most cases, make your selector more specific to get your style applied. For instance, if `#header p{}` doesn't work, then you can try adding a `#header #subheader p{}` ID, a `#header p.head{}` class, and so on.

When Cascade and !important rules do not give a conclusive answer, specificity calculation seems to be a hard and time-consuming job. Although *Less* won't help you here, tools such as Firebug (and other developer tools) can make the specificity visible. An example using Firebug is shown in the following screenshot, where the selector with the highest specificity is displayed at the top of the screen and the overruled styles are struck out:

```
Inherited from ul.nav

.bs-sidenav {                                    docs.css (line 462)
    .text-shadow: 0 1px 0 #FFFFFF;
}

.nav {                                    bootstrap.min.css (line 7)
    list-style: none outside none;
}

Inherited from body

body {                                    bootstrap.min.css (line 7)
    color: #333333;
    font-family: "Helvetica Neue",Helvetica,Arial,sans-serif;
    font-size: 14px;
    line-height: 1.42857;
}

Inherited from html

html {                                    bootstrap.min.css (line 7)
    font-size: 62.5%;
}

html {                                    bootstrap.min.css (line 7)
    font-family: sans-serif;
}
```

An example of specificity in Firebug

Building your layouts with flexible boxes

The **Flexbox Layout** (also called flexible boxes) is a new feature of CSS3. It is extremely useful in creating responsive and flexible layouts. Flexbox provides the ability to dynamically change the layout for different screen resolutions. It does not use floats and contains margins that do not collapse with their content. Unfortunately, major browsers do not offer full support for Flexbox layouts at this moment. We focus on Flexbox due to its power, and as it is an important feature of CSS, we can also produce and maintain it using *Less*. You can access a set of *Less* mixins for CSS3 Flexbox at https://gist.github.com/bassjobsen/8068034. You can use these mixins to create Flexbox layouts with *Less*, without using duplicate code.

These mixins will not be explained in great detail now, but the following example shows how *Less* reduces the code needed to create a flex container. Using CSS, you might use the following code:

```
div#wrapper {
    display: -webkit-flex;
    display: -moz-flex;
    display: -ms-flexbox;
    display: -ms-flex;
    display: flex;
}
```

Downloading the example code

You can download the example code files for all Packt books you have purchased from your account at http://www.packtpub.com/. If you purchased this book elsewhere, you can visit http://www.packtpub.com/support/ and register to have the files e-mailed directly to you.

However, if you use *Less*, the same effect can be produced by inserting the following line of code:

```
div#wrapper { .flex-display; }
```

You can use Google Chrome to test your Flexbox layouts. At the time of writing this book, Firefox and Internet Explorer IE11 also offered full or better support for Flexbox layouts. Flexboxes have been mentioned because they have the potential to play an important role in the future of web design. For now, they are beyond the scope of this book. This book will focus on creating responsive and flexible layouts with *Less* using CSS media queries and grids.

Please visit https://developer.mozilla.org/en-US/docs/Web/Guide/CSS/Flexible_boxes for additional information, examples, and browser compatibility.

Compiling Less

After delving into the theory of CSS, you can finally start using *Less*. As mentioned earlier, it has the same syntax as CSS. This means any CSS code is, in fact, a valid *Less* code too. With *Less*, you can produce CSS code that can be used to style your website. The process used to make CSS from *Less* is called **compiling**, where you can compile *Less* code via the **server side** or **client side**. The examples given in this book will make use of client-side compiling. Client side, in this context, means loading the code in a browser and compiling *Less* code into CSS code using resources from the local machine. Client-side compiling is used in this book because it is the easiest way to get started while being good enough for developing your *Less* skills.

It is important to note that the results from client-side compiling serve only for demonstration purposes. For production and especially when considering the performance of an application, it is recommended that you use server-side **precompiling**. *Less* bundles a compiler based on **Node.js**, and many other GUI's are available to precompile your code. These GUI's will be discussed towards the end of this chapter.

Getting started with Less

You can finally start using *Less*. The first thing you have to do is download *Less* from `http://www.lesscss.org/`. In this book, Version 1.6 of `less.js` will be used. After downloading it, an HTML5 document should be created. It should include `less.js` and your very first *Less* file.

Please note that you can download the examples, including a copy of `less.js`, from the support files for this chapter in the downloadable files for the book on `www.packtpub.com`.

To start with, have a look at this plain yet well-structured HTML5 file:

```
<!doctype html>
<html lang="en">
<head>
  <meta charset="utf-8">

  <title>Example code</title>
  <meta name="description" content="Example code">
  <meta name="author" content="Bass Jobsen">

  <link rel="stylesheet/less" type="text/css"
    href="less/styles.less" />
   <script src="less.js" type="text/javascript"></script>
</head>

<body>
<h1>Less makes me Happy!</h1>
</body>
</html>
```

As you can see, a *Less* file has been added to this document using the following code:

```
<link rel="stylesheet/less" type="text/css"
  href="less/styles.less" />
```

When `rel="stylesheet/less"` is used, the code will be the same as for a style sheet. After the *Less* file, you can call `less.js` using the following code:

```
<script src="less.js" type="text/javascript"></script>
```

In fact, that's all that you need to get started!

To keep things clear, `html5shiv` (which you can access at `http://code.google.com/p/html5shiv/`) and **Modernizr** (which you can access at `http://modernizr.com/`) have been ignored for now. These scripts add support and detection of new CSS3 and HTML5 features for older browsers such as IE7 and IE8. It is expected that you will be using a modern browser such as Mozilla Firefox, Google Chrome, or any version of Internet Explorer beyond IE8. These will offer full support of HTML5, CSS3, and **media queries**, which you will need when reading this book and doing the exercises.

> You already know you should only use `less.js` for development and testing in most cases; there can still be use cases which do justice to the client-side use of `less.js` in production. To support `less.js` for older browsers, you could try es5-shim (`https://github.com/es-shims/es5-shim/`).

Now, open `http://localhost/index.html` in your browser. You will see the **Less makes me Happy!** header text in its default font and color. After this, you should open `less/styles.less` in your favorite text editor. The syntax of *Less* and CSS doesn't differ here, so you can enter the following code into this file:

```
h1{color:red;}
```

Following this, reload your browser. You should see the header text in red.

From the preceding code, `h1` is the selector that selects the HTML `H1` attribute in your HTML. The `color` property has been set to `red` between the accolades. The properties will then be applied onto your selectors, just like CSS does.

> It is not necessary to have a web server that is running. Navigating to `index.html` on your hard drive with your browser should be enough. Unfortunately, this won't work for all browsers, so use Mozilla Firefox in order to be sure. The examples in this book use `http://localhost/map/`, but this can be replaced with something similar to `file:///map/` or `c:\map\`, depending on your situation.

Using the watch function for automatic reloading

The less.js file has a **watch** function, which checks your files for changes and reloads your browser views when they are found. It is pretty simple to use. Execute the following steps:

1. Add #!watch after the URL you want to open.

2. Add #!watch after index.html and then reload the browser window.

3. So, open http://localhost/index.html#!watch in your browser and start editing your *Less* files. Your browser will reflect your changes without having to reload.

4. Now open less/styles.less in your text editor. In this file, write #h1{color:red;} and then save the file.

5. You should now navigate to your browser, which should show **Less makes me Happy!** in red.

6. Rearrange your screen in order to see both the text editor and browser together in the same window.

7. Furthermore, if you change red to blue in less/styles.less, you will see that the browser tracks these changes and shows **Less makes me Happy!** in blue once the file is saved.

Pretty cool, isn't it?

> The examples in this code use color names instead of hexadecimal values. For example, the code uses red instead of #ff0000. The basic color names are converted to their hexadecimal value by less.js and written to the CSS. In this book, named colors are always used.

Debugging your code

As we are only human, we are prone to making a mistake or a typo. It is important to be able to see what you did wrong and debug your code. If your *Less* file contains errors, it won't compile at all. So, one small typo breaks the complete style of the document.

Debugging is also easy with less.js. To use debugging or allow less.js to display errors, you can add the following line of code to your index.html:

```
<link rel="stylesheet/less" type="text/css" href="less/styles.less" />
<script type="text/javascript">less = { env: 'development' };</script>
<script src="less.js" type="text/javascript"></script>
```

As you can see, the line with less = { env: 'development' }; is new here. This line contains less as a JavaScript variable used by less.js. In fact, this is a global *Less* object used to parse some settings to less.js. The only setting that will be used in this book is env: 'development'. For more settings, check out the following website: http://lesscss.org/#client-side-usage-browser-options.

 env: 'development' also prevents *Less* from caching. Less doesn't cache files in the browser cache. Instead, files are cached in the browser's local storage. If env is set to production, this caching could yield unexpected results as the changed and saved files are not compiled.

To try this new setting, edit less/styles.less again and remove an accolade to create an invalid syntax of the h1{color:red form and then save the file.

In your browser, you will see a page like the following screenshot:

ParseError: missing closing `}`

in <u>styles.less</u> on line 2, column 1:

```
1   p{color:red;
2
```

An example of a Less parse error

Besides **syntax errors**, there will also be **name errors** that are displayed. In the case of a name error, an undeclared function or variable would have been used.

It is possible to set other settings for debugging, either in the global *Less* object or by appending the setting to the URL. For example, you can specify the dumpLineNumbers setting by adding the following lines of code to your HTML file:

```
<script type="text/javascript">less = { env:
  'development',dumpLineNumbers: "mediaQuery"
};</script>
```

Alternatively, you can add !dumpLineNumbers:mediaQuery to the URL. This setting enables other tools to find the line number of the error in the *Less* source file. Setting this option to mediaQuery makes error reporting available for the FireBug or Chrome development tools. Similarly, setting this to comments achieves the same for tools such as FireLess. For instance, using FireLess allows Firebug to display the original *Less* filename and the line number of CSS styles generated by *Less*.

FireBug, Chrome development tools, or the default browser inspect the element functions (which you can access by right-clicking on your browser screen) can also be used to see and evaluate the compiled CSS. The CSS is displayed as inline CSS wrapped inside a <style type="text/css" id="less:book-less-styles"> tag. In the example given in the following screenshot, you will see an ID with value less:book-less-styles. The value of this ID have been automatically generated by *Less* based on the path and name of the book/less/styles.less *Less* file:

```
<style id="less:book-less-styles" type="text/css">
1   p {
2       color: navy;
3   }
</style>
```

Less-generated CSS styles

Example code used in this book

In this book, you will find many code examples. Unless explicitly mentioned, the format of these examples always shows the *Less* code first, followed by the compiled CSS code. For instance, you can write the following lines of code in *Less*:

```
mixin() {
color: green;
}
p {
.mixin();
}
```

This code will be compiled into the following CSS syntax :

```
p {
color: green;
}
```

Your first layout in Less

You must first open `first.html` (from the downloadable files for the book) in your browser and then open `less/first.less` in your text editor. In your browser, you will see a representation of a header, body, and footer.

As expected, `less/first.less` contains the *Less* code that will be converted into valid CSS by the `less.js` compiler. Any error in this file will stop the compiler and throw an error. Although the *Less* code shows some similarities to the plain CSS code, the process described here totally differs from editing your CSS directly.

The following screenshot shows you how this layout will look when opened in your web browser:

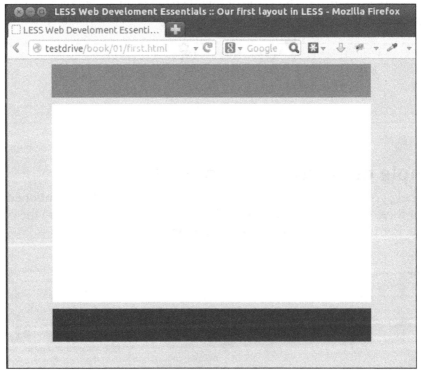

Your first layout in Less

Vendor-specific rules

CSS3 introduced **vendor-specific rules**, which offer you the possibility of writing some additional CSS applicable for only one browser. At first sight, this seems the exact opposite of what you want. What you want is a set of standards and practicalities that work the same with every browser and a standard set of HTML and CSS which has the same effect and interpretation for every browser. These vendor-specific rules are intended to help us reach this utopia. Vendor-specific rules also provide us with early implementations of standard properties and alternative syntax. Last but not least, these rules allow browsers to implement proprietary **CSS properties** that would otherwise have no working standard (and may never actually become the standard).

For these reasons, vendor-specific rules play an important role in many new features of CSS3. For example, **animation properties**, **border-radius**, and **box-shadow** all depend on vendor-specific rules.

Vendors use the following prefixes:

- **WebKit**: `-webkit`
- **Firefox**: `-moz`
- **Opera**: `-o`
- **Internet Explorer**: `-ms`

Build rounded corners with border-radius

Border-radius is a new CSS3 property which will make many web developers happy. With border-radius, you can give HTML elements a rounded corner. In previous years, many implementations of rounded corners using images and transparency have been seen. However, these were inflexible (not fluid) and difficult to maintain.

Vendor-specific rules are required for implementation, and although rounded corners can't be handled with a single line of code, its usage definitely makes rounding corners a lot easier.

To give an element rounded corners with a radius of 10 pixels, you can use the CSS code with vendor-specific rules as follows:

```
-webkit-border-radius: 10px;
-moz-border-radius: 10px;
border-radius: 10px;
```

For rounded corners with different radii, use a list with values separated by spaces: `10 px 5px 20px 15px;`. The radii are given in the following order: top-left, top-right, bottom-right, and bottom-left. By keeping these rules in mind, you will see how *Less* can keep your code clean.

You can open `roundedcorners.html` from the download section of this chapter in your browser, and open `less/roundedcorners.less` in your text editor. In your browser, you will see a representation of a header, body, and footer with rounded corners.

The CSS for the header in `less/roundedcorners.less` looks like the following code:

```
#header{
background-color: red;
-webkit-border-radius: 10px;
-moz-border-radius: 10px;
border-radius: 10px;
}
```

You can see that using vendor-specific rules, the corners have been created with a radius of 10 pixels. If you were using CSS, you would have to repeat the vendor-specific rules three times for the header, footer, and body. In order to change these rules or add a vendor, you would also have to change the same code three times. To begin with, you will perhaps think, "Why not group the selectors?", in a fashion similar to the following code:

```
#header, #content, #footer{
-webkit-border-radius: 10px;
-moz-border-radius: 10;
border-radius: 10px;
}
```

The preceding code is syntactically correct in order to write CSS or *Less* code, but as your code base grows, it won't be easy to maintain. Grouping selectors based on properties makes no sense when reading and maintaining your code. Such constructs will also introduce many duplicated and unstructured usages of the same selectors.

With *Less*, you are able to solve these problems efficiently. By creating a so-called **mixin**, you can solve the issues mentioned earlier. For the border radius, you can use the following code:

```
.roundedcornersmixin()
{
-webkit-border-radius: 10px;
-moz-border-radius: 10px;
border-radius: 10px;
}
```

To use this mixin, you will call it as a property for the selector using the following code:

```
#header{
background-color: red;
.roundedcornersmixin();
}
```

The compiled CSS of this *Less* code will now be as follows:

```
#header{
background-color: red;
-webkit-border-radius: 10px;
-moz-border-radius: 10px;
border-radius: 10px;
}
```

Looking at the original code in the less/roundedcorners.less file, you can see that the preceding code wouldn't be able to work for #content. The border radius for the content is 20 pixels instead of 10 pixels, as used for the header and footer. Again, *Less* helps us solve this efficiently. Mixins can be called with parameters in the same way in which functions can be called in functional programming. This means that in combination with a value and a reference for this value, mixins can be called in order to set the properties. In this example, this will change to the following code:

```
.roundedcornersmixin(@radius: 10px) {
-webkit-border-radius: @radius;
-moz-border-radius: @radius;
border-radius: @radius;
}
```

In the .roundedcornersmixin(@radius: 10px) mixin, @radius is our parameter, and its default value will be 10px.

From this point onwards, mixins can be used in your code. The .roundedcornersmixin(50px); statement will set the corners with a radius of 50px and the .roundedcornersmixin(); statement will do the same with a radius of 10px (default).

Using this, you can rewrite less/roundedcorners.less so that it changes to the following code:

```
/* mixins */
.roundedcornersmixin(@radius: 10px) {
-webkit-border-radius: @radius;
-moz-border-radius: @radius;
border-radius: @radius;
```

```
}
#header{
background-color: red;
.roundedcornersmixin();
}
#content{
background-color: white;
min-height: 300px;
.roundedcornersmixin(20px);
}
#footer{
background-color: navy;
.roundedcornersmixin();
}
```

 The `less/roundedcornersmixins.less` file from the downloads section contains a copy of this code. To use this, you also have to change the reference in your HTML file to `<link rel="stylesheet/less" type="text/css" href="less/groundedcornersmixins.less" />`.

Note that this code leaves out the general styling of the `div` and `body` tags in the HTML. These styles are only used to make the demo look good and do not actually demonstrate *Less* in any useful manner.

After rewriting your *Less* code, reload your browser or watch it if you have applied the `#!watch` trick. You will see that the output will be exactly the same. This shows you how to get the same results with *Less* using a more efficiently structured code.

Preventing cross-browser issues with CSS resets

When talking about **cascade** in CSS, there will no doubt be a mention of the browser default settings getting a higher precedence than the author's preferred styling. When writing *Less* code, you will overwrite the browser's default styling. In other words, anything that you do not define will be assigned a default styling, which is defined by the browser. This behavior plays a major role in many cross-browser issues. To prevent these sorts of problems, you can perform a **CSS reset**. The most famous browser reset is Eric Meyer's CSS Reset (accessible at `http://meyerweb.com/eric/tools/css/reset/`).

CSS resets overwrite the default styling rules of the browser and create a starting point for styling. This starting point looks and acts the same on all (or most) browsers. In this book, normalize.css v2 is used. Normalize.css is a modern, HTML5-ready alternative to CSS resets and can be downloaded from `http://necolas.github.io/normalize.css/`. It lets browsers render all elements more consistently and makes them adhere to modern standards.

To use a CSS reset, you can make use of the `@import` directive of *Less*. With `@import`, you can include other *Less* files in your main *Less* file. The syntax is `@import "{filename}";`. By default, the search path for the directives starts at the directory of the main file. Although setting alternative search paths is possible (by setting the path's variable of your *Less* environment), it will not be used in this book.

The example *Less* files in this book will contain `@import "normalize.less";` in the first few lines of the code. Again, you should note that `normalize.less` does contain the CSS code. You should pay particular attention to the profits of this solution!

If you want to change or update the CSS reset, you will only have to replace one file. If you have to manage or build more than one project, which most of you should be doing, then you can simply reuse the complete reset code.

Creating background gradients

A new feature in CSS3 is the possibility of adding a **gradient** in the background color of an element. This acts as a replacement for complex code and image fallbacks.

It is possible to define different types of gradient and use two or more colors. In the following figure, you will see a background gradient of different colors:

A gradient example (from `W3schools.com`)

In the next example, you can use a linear gradient of two colors. The background gradients use vendor-specific rules.

You can make use of the example code from the rounded corners example to add gradients to it.

The first step is to copy or open `less/gradient.less` and add a new mixin at the start of this file as shown in the following code:

```
/* Mixin */
.gradient (@start: black, @stop: white,@origin: left) {
    background-color: @start;
```

```
background-image: -webkit-linear-gradient(@origin, @start,
    @stop);
  background-image: -moz-linear-gradient(@origin, @start,
    @stop);
background-image: -o-linear-gradient(@origin, @start, @stop);
background-image: -ms-linear-gradient(@origin, @start, @stop);
background-image: linear-gradient(@origin, @start, @stop);
}
```

This will create gradients from the left (`@origin`) to the right with colors from `@start` to `@stop`. This mixin has default values.

IE9 (and its earlier versions) do not support gradients. A fallback can be added by adding `background-color: @start;`, which will create a uniform colored background for older browsers.

After adding the mixin to your code, you can call on it for our #header, #body, and #footer selectors as shown in the following code:

```
#header{
background-color: red;
.roundedcornersmixin();
.gradient(red,lightred);
}
#content{
background-color: white;
min-height: 300px;
.roundedcornersmixin(20px);
.gradient();
}
#footer{
background-color: navy;
.roundedcornersmixin(20px);
.gradient(navy,lightblue);
}
```

For example, if you renamed the *Less* file to `less/gradient.less`, you would have also had to change the reference in your HTML file to the following code:

```
<link rel="stylesheet/less" type="text/css"
  href="less/gradient.less" />
```

If you now load the HTML file in the browser, your results should be like the following screenshot:

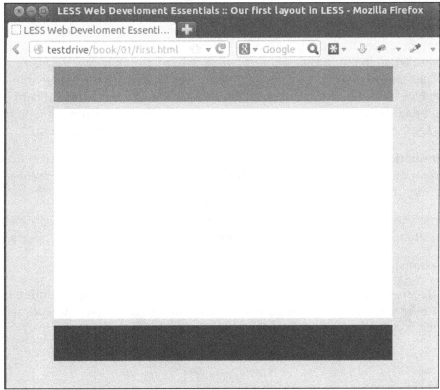

Gradients in the header, content, and footer from the example code

CSS transitions, transformations, and animations

Another new feature in CSS3 is the presence of transitions, transformations, and animations. These functions can replace the animated images, flash animations, and JavaScripts in the existing or new web pages. The difference between transitions, transforms, and animations isn't trivial. **Animations** are constructed with a range of `@keyframes`, where each `@keyframes` handles different states of your element in time. **Transitions** also describe the state of element between start and end. Transitions are mostly triggered by CSS changes, such as a mouse over (hover) of an element.

To make things clear, it is important to keep in mind the button that is about to be pressed. The button will have two states: pressed and not pressed. Without transitions and animations, we are enabled to style these states only. The color of the button is white, and its color becomes red when you hover the mouse over it. (In CSS terms, its state becomes hovered by adding the `:hover` pseudo class.) In this case, the transition describes how the hovered button becomes red. For example, the change in color from white to red in two seconds (which makes it pink halfway) shows that the start of the color change is slow and changes faster as time passes. Using animations here enables us to describe the state of the button for every time interval between the start and end. For example, you don't have to change the color from white to red, but the change covers all the states, from white, blue, green, and finally to red.

Transformations change the position of an element and how it looks. They do not depend on the state of the element. Some of the possible transformations are **scaling**, **translating** (moving), and **rotating**.

In practice, we use a combination of animations, transformations, and/or transitions in most situations. Also, in this case, vendor-specific rules will play an important role.

Now, a transformation will be added to our example.

Using the example code with rounded corners and gradients, copy the following code to `less/transition.less` or open `less/transition.less` and add the following code to the beginning of the file:

```
/* Mixin */
.transition (@prop: all, @time: 1s, @ease: linear) {
-webkit-transition: @prop @time @ease;
-moz-transition: @prop @time @ease;
-o-transition: @prop @time @ease;
-ms-transition: @prop @time @ease;
transition: @prop @time @ease;
}
```

This **mixin** has three variables; the first will be the **property** (`@prop`) that you will change. This can be `height`, `background-color`, `visibility`, and so on. The default value `all` shouldn't be used in the production code as this will have a negative effect on performance. `@time` sets the duration in milliseconds or seconds with `s` appended to it. The last variable, `@ease`, sets the **transition-timing-function property**. This function describes the value of a property, given that a certain percentage of it has been completed. The transition-timing-function property describes the completeness of the transition as a function of time. Setting it to `linear` shows the effect with the same speed from start to end, while `ease` starts slow and ends slow, having a higher speed in the middle. The predefined functions are `ease`, `linear`, `ease-in`, `ease-out`, `ease-in-out`, `step-start`, and `step-end`.

Now, you can edit less/transition.less to use this **mixin**. You can set the background color of the body when you hover over it. Note that you don't need to use the transition to change the gradient color but rather change the background-color attribute. You are using background-color because transition-duration doesn't have a visible effect on the gradient. The code of the background-color transition is as follows:

```
#content{
background-color: white;
min-height: 300px;
.roundedcornersmixin(20px);
.transition(background-color,5s);
}
#content:hover{
background-color: red;
}
```

If you renamed the *Less* file, for example, to less/transition.less, you would also have to change the reference in your HTML file to the following code:

```
<link rel="stylesheet/less" type="text/css"
  href="less/transition.less" />
```

If you load the HTML file in the browser, you will be able to see the results in the browser. Move your mouse over the content and see it change from white to red in 5 seconds.

Finally, a second example that rotates the header can be added. In this example, you will use @keyframes. Using @keyframes will be complex. So, in this case, you can define some vendor-specific rules and add these animation properties to #header: as follows:

```
@-moz-keyframes spin { 100% { -moz-transform: rotate(360deg); } }
@-webkit-keyframes spin { 100% { -webkit-transform:
  rotate(360deg); } }
@keyframes spin { 100% { -webkit-transform: rotate(360deg);
  transform:rotate(360deg); } }
#header{
    -webkit-animation:spin 4s linear infinite;
    -moz-animation:spin 4s linear infinite;
    animation:spin 4s linear infinite;
}
```

You can add the preceding code to our example files or open `less/keyframes.less`.

If you renamed the *Less* file, for example, to `less/keyframes.less`, you also have to change the reference in your HTML file to the following code:

```
<link rel="stylesheet/less" type="text/css"
href="less/keyframes.less" />
```

Now, load the HTML file in the browser and watch your results. Amazing, isn't it? With a little bit of creative thinking, you will see the possibilities of creating a rotating windmill or a winking owl using only CSS3. However, the first thing that should be done is to explain the code used here in more detail. As mentioned earlier, there are many cases in which you would make combinations of **animations** and **transformations**. In this example, you also get to animate a transformation effect. To understand what is going on, the code can be split into three parts.

The first part is `@keyframes`, shown in the following code, which describe the value of the CSS properties (transformation in this case) as a function of the percentage of the **animation** completeness:

```
@keyframes spin { 100% { -webkit-transform: rotate(360deg);
transform:rotate(360deg); } }
```

These **keyframes** have been given the name reference `spin`, which is not a special effect but only a chosen name. In the preceding example, a state of 100 percent completeness is described. At this state, the animated element should have made a rotation of 360 degrees.

This rotation is the second part that needs our attention. The **transformation** describes the position or dimensions of an element in the space. In this example, the position is described by the number of degrees of rotation around the axis, 360 degrees at 100 percent, 180 degrees at 50 percent, 90 degrees at 25 percent, and so on.

The third part is the animation itself, described by: `animation:spin 4s linear infinite;`. This is the shorthand notation of settings of the subproperties of the animation property. In fact, you can write this as the following code, without the vendor-specific rules:

```
animation-name: spin;
animation-duration: 4s;
animation-timing-function:linear;
animation-iteration-count:  infinite;
```

You can use these three parts to build a complete animation. After doing this, you can extend it. For example, add an extra keyframe, which makes the time curve nonlinear, as follows:

```
@keyframes spin {
50% { transform: rotate(10deg);}
100% {transform: rotate(360deg); }
  }
```

You can add a second property using `background-color`. Don't forget to remove the gradient to see its effect. This is shown in the following code:

```
@-moz-keyframes spin {
50% { transform: rotate(10deg); background-color:green;}
100% { transform: rotate(360deg); }
  }
//.gradient(red,yellow);
```

You will have noticed that the complete profit of using *Less* isn't realized here. You will have to write the `@keyframes` definition repeatedly due to its variable animation name. In *Chapter 4, Avoid Reinventing the Wheel*, a solution will be provided to you for this.

Unfortunately, browser support for transitions, transformations, and animations is not great and varies between browsers. Google Chrome does not support CSS 3D transforms, Firefox lacks support for CSS Filters, and IE9 (and earlier versions) don't support them at all. To solve this, many developers look to jQuery to support their animations. The `jQuery.animate()` function allows us to change the CSS properties of the elements using JavaScript. You can still use *Less* to set the initial CSS. An alternative for this will be to use `animate.css` (which you can access at `https://github.com/daneden/animate.css`); this cross-browser library of CSS animations gets converted into *Less* code with a jQuery fallback.

Box-sizing

The **box-sizing** property is the one that sets the CSS-box model used for calculating the dimensions of an element. In fact, box-sizing is not new in CSS, but nonetheless, switching your code to `box-sizing: border-box` will make your work a lot easier. When using the `border-box` settings, calculation of the width of an element includes border width and padding. So, changing the border of padding won't break your layouts. You can find a copy of the code used in this section in `boxsizing.html` from the download files.

Nowadays, most web designs use a grid. Grids split your design into columns of equal size. This helps you make things clear and build responsive interfaces. Depending on the available screen size (or width), you can show your content and navigation with a different representation of the same columns.

To handle different screen sizes, some parts of your website will have fluid width or height. Other elements, such as borders, gutters, and the white space, should have a fixed width. The combination of fluid widths as a percentage of the screen width (or viewport) with fixed widths becomes complex. This complexity will be due to the fact that browsers use different calculations for padding and margins of elements.

In order for you to see this, look at the following example. A container of 500 pixels width has been created. Inside this container, you can add two rows and split the second row into two parts of 50 percent (or half) width.

```
<div class="wrapper" style="width:300px;">
  <div style="background-color:red;width;100%;">1</div>
  <div style="background-
    color:green;width:50%;float:left;">2</div>
  <div style="background-
    color:blue;width:50%;float:right;">3</div>
</div>
```

This will now look like the following screenshot:

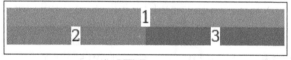

An HTML wrapper

The current structure doesn't show a problem until you add some padding, which is used to construct some space or a border between the two columns on the second row (numbers 2 and 3 in the image of the HTML wrapper). The padding and the border will break our layout as follows:

```
<div class="wrapper" style="width:300px;">
<div style="background-color:red;width:100%;">1</div>
<div style="background-color:green;width:50%;float:left;border:5px
solid yellow;">2</div>
<div style="background-color:blue;width:50%;border:5px solid
yellow;float:right;">3</div>
</div>
<br>
<div class="wrapper" style="width:300px;">
<div style="background-color:red;width;100%;">1</div>
```

```
<div style="background-color:green;float:left;width:50%;padding-
right:5px;"><div style="background-color:yellow;">2</div></div>
<div style="background-color:blue;width:50%;padding-
right:5px;float:right;">3</div>
</div>
```

Finally, the output of this code should look like the following screenshot:

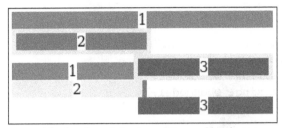

A broken layout due to padding and borders

A similar action can be performed, except that the wrappers can be wrapped inside an extra wrapper. The `box-sizing: border-box;` declaration can then be applied to this. Now, the results should look like the following screenshot:

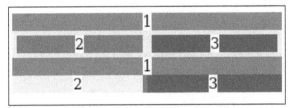

A layout with box-sizing: border-box

As you can see, the padding and borders are subtracted by 50 percent from the parent. This will make the calculation a lot easier. Of course, you can do the calculating yourself once the parent container wrapper has a fixed width. If the parent has 300 pixels, then 50 percent of this will be 150 pixels. Taking away the padding and the width of the border will give you the fixed size of a column. This won't work when your parent has a fluid width (the percentage of the viewport). Fluid layouts change their width with the width of the screen. If your screen becomes smaller, then all the elements become smaller too and the percentage stays equal. By doing calculations for all the possible screen sizes to find the real size of a column that allows all of your elements to align, you will quickly find this to be a long, challenging, and arduous process.

For these reasons, you should make use of `box-sizing: border-box;` for all the examples in this book. Please note that box-sizing has to also be defined by vendor-specific rules as follows:

```
-webkit-box-sizing: border-box;
-moz-box-sizing: border-box;
box-sizing: border-box;
```

In this example, the *Less* code will be as follows:

```
// Box sizing mixin
.box-sizing(@boxmodel) {
  -webkit-box-sizing: @boxmodel;
    -moz-box-sizing: @boxmodel;
         box-sizing: @boxmodel;
}
// Reset the box-sizing
*,
*:before,
*:after {
  .box-sizing(border-box);
}
```

> This code has been added into a separate file called `boxsizing.less`. From now on, the basics of our *Less* files will now contain the following code:
>
> ```
> @import: "normalize.less";
> @import: "boxsizing.less";
> ```

In the following chapters, you will learn more about organizing your *Less* code into files.

Server-side compiling

You have taken the first few steps towards *Less* development already. As explained earlier, client-side compiling has been used. However, **client-side** compiling with `less.js` shouldn't be used on real websites. This is because despite making your development easy and fast, compiling your *Less* files for every page request (or in fact, initial page load per user) will actually slow down your website.

For the production environment, it is required that you compile your files and serve the final CSS file to the browser. The term **server side** can be somewhat misleading. Server side in this context means a compiled CSS code is sent to the client's browser instead of *Less* code, which has to be compiled in the client's browser by less.js before it is shown. You should precompile your *Less* code. By copying and pasting the results of *less.js* to a file and including this as a CSS file in your HTML files, you should have the same effect, except that your CSS is not minimized.

Less bundles a command-line compiler. Installing and using it is simple using the following command:

```
>> npm install -g less
>> lessc styles.less styles.css
```

The package manager for the Node JavaScript platform is **npm**. Node enables you to run Java scripts without a browser. Node and npm run on Windows, Mac OS X, and other Unix/*nix machines. You will find the Node.js source code or a prebuilt installer for your platform by visiting `http://nodejs.org/download/`. To install npm, please read the instructions in the README file by visiting `https://www.npmjs.org/doc/README.html`.

Use the `-help` function to get a list of options you can use with the following command-line compiler:

```
>> lessc -help
```

`lessc styles.less styles.css` compiles `styles.less` to `styles.css`. The links to `styles.css` in your HTML after successfully compiling it are then shown as follows:

```
<link rel="stylesheet/css" type="text/css" href="styles.css">
```

Compressing and minimizing your CSS

After compilation, the CSS code is clean and readable. When taking this code into production, you have to compress and minimize it in order to increase the loading speed and save on the bandwidth as well. The basic steps for **compressing** and **minimizing** the CSS code are removing comments, white spaces, and other unnecessary code. The results won't be easy to be read by a human, but this doesn't matter because you can use the *Less* files to update or modify the CSS.

The *Less* command-line compiler has two options for compressing and minimizing. The first option (**-x** or –yui-compress) uses the **YUI CSS Compressor** (which you can access at http://yui.github.io/yuicompressor/css.html) and the second option (--clean-css) uses **clean-css** (which you can access at https://github.com/GoalSmashers/clean-css). You cannot use both options together. **Clean-css** claims to be faster, and until recently, you would not have found much difference in the compression. By compiling keyframes.less from the previous example, including normalize.less and boxsizing.less, the result will have a size of 4377 bytes. With clean-css, this drops to 3516 bytes, whilst YUI gives 3538 bytes. Since Version 1.5.0 of *Less*, clean-css is the compiler's default option.

Graphical user interfaces

Some of you will prefer a **Graphical User Interface** (GUI) instead of command-line compiling. There are many GUIs available for different platforms in order to edit and compile your *Less* code. All of them cannot be mentioned here. Instead, the following is a list of the most positive noticeable ones:

- WinLess is a Windows GUI for less.js.
- SimpLESS is a cross-platform editor and compiler with many functions, including the automatic addintion of vendor-specific rules to your code.
- CodeKIT is a GUI for Mac (OS X). It compiles many languages including *Less*. It includes optimizations and browser previews.
- The last one mentioned is Crunch! Crunch! is also a cross-platform compiler and editor.

When choosing a GUI for *Less* development, always check which version of less.js it uses. Some GUI's are built on older versions of less.js and don't support the latest features.

Web developers using Visual Studio should check out **Web Essentials**. Web Essentials extends Visual Studio with a lot of new features, including *Less*. Also, other IDEs such as **PHPStorm** have built-in *Less* compilers. There is a *Less* plugin for **Eclipse** also.

Summary

In this chapter, you refreshed and extended your knowledge about CSS3. You learned how to compile your *Less* code on the client side. Furthermore, you have written the code that allows you to have rounded corners, gradients, and animations in *Less*, so you can now witness the profits of using *Less* and take the crucial initial steps to organize and plan your new projects. You witnessed why you would want to use CSS resets, how to compile these into *Less* code, as well as how the box-sizing border-box can make your job easier. You also saw what a mixin is, how to use it, and how you can import a *Less* file with the `@import` directive. Last but not least, you have learned what server-side compiling is and how to use GUIs.

In the next chapter, you will learn how to use variables in *Less* and how to build and use complex mixins.

2
Using Variables and Mixins

In this chapter, you will study *Less* in more detail, where you will learn more about variables and mixins. **Variables** in *Less* can be reused anywhere in the code. Although they are often defined in a single place, they can also be overwritten elsewhere in the code. They are used to define commonly used values that can be edited only once at a single place. Based on the **Don't Repeat Yourself** (**DRY**) principle, commonly used values will help you build websites that are easier to maintain. **Mixins** are used to set the properties of a class. They bundle tasks in a single line of code and are also reusable. You will learn how to create, use, and reuse them in your project and write better CSS without code duplications.

This chapter will cover the following topics:

- Commenting on your code
- Using variables
- Escaping values
- Using mixins

Comments

Comments make your code clear and readable for others. It is important that you are able to understand them clearly. That is why this chapter starts with some notes and examples of comments.

 Don't be sparse with your comments when keeping the file size, download time, and performance in mind. In the process of compiling and minimizing your final CSS code, comments and other layout structures will be effectively removed. You can add comments for understanding and readability wherever needed.

In *Less*, you can add comments in the same way as you did while writing the CSS code. Comment lines are placed between /* */. *Less* also allows single-line comments that start with //.

Using *Less*, you will conserve these comments in the final style sheet apart from the single-line comments, which are not printed. **Minimizers** will remove these comments in your final **compiled style sheet**. An example of this can be seen in the following code:

```
/* comments by Bass
.mixins() { ~"this mixin is commented out"; }
*/
```

Nested comments

Although *Less*, like PHP or JavaScript, doesn't allow nested comments, single-line comments that start with // are allowed and can be mixed with the normal comment syntax. This is shown in the following code snippet:

```
/*
//commented out
*/
```

Special comments

Minimizers define a special comment syntax, sometimes to allow an important comment, such as a license notice, to be included in the minimized output as well. You can use this syntax to write some copyright notices at the top of your style sheet. Using clean CSS and the default minimizer of the `clean-css` command-line compiler of *Less*, you should place this important command between /*! !*/, as shown in the following example code:

```
/*!
very important comment!
        !*/
```

Variables

Variables in *Less* help you keep your files organized and easy to maintain. They allow you to specify widely-used values in a single place and then reuse them throughout your *Less* code. The properties of the final style sheet can be set with variables. So, imagine that you don't have to search for every declaration of a specific color or value in your style sheets any more. How does all of this work? Variables will start with @ and have a name. Examples of such variables include `@color`, `@size`, and `@tree`. To write the name, you are allowed to use any alphanumeric character, underscores, and dashes. This means that `@this-is-variable-name-with-35-chars` is a valid variable name.

> Although alphanumeric characters, underscores, and dashes are used in variable names in this book, the specifications allow you to use any character, with a few exceptions. The specifications find their origin in the CSS grammar (which you can view at http://www.w3.org/TR/CSS21/grammar.html). Names starting with a dash are reserved for vendor-specific rules, and a space is already used to separate class names from each other. It is possible and allowed to use escaping, which is very rare for (programming) languages. However, the escaping of white spaces is not possible. NULL is also not allowed.

Unfortunately, the use of @ is ambiguous in *Less*. As you have seen in the first chapter, parameters used by mixins also start with @. That's not all. As valid CSS code is also valid *Less* code, there will be CSS media query declarations that also start with @. The context will make it clear when @ is used to declare a variable. If the context is not clear enough, the meaning of the @ will be explicitly mentioned in this book.

You can give a variable a value, which will be called a declaration. A value can contain anything that is a valid value for a CSS property.

You can use a colon (:) to assign a value to a variable. A declaration ends with a semicolon (;). The following examples will make this clear:

```
@width: 10px;
@color: blue;
@list: a b c d;
@csv-list: a, b, c, d;
@escaped-value: ~"dark@{color}";
```

After the declaration of a variable, you can use the variable anywhere in your code to reference its value. This quality makes variables extremely powerful when programming *Less* code. Take a look at the example code for this chapter from the downloadable code for this book to get a better understanding.

Organizing your files

As you have seen, you only have to declare a variable once to use it anywhere in the code. So, to make changes to the variables, you also have to change them only once. The example code defines the variables in a separate file called less/variables. less. It is a great practice to organize your files. If you want to change something, you now know where to look.

Recalling **CSS reset** and **border-boxing** from the first chapter, your main *Less* file will now look like the following code snippet:

```
@import "less/normalize.less";
@import "less/boxsizing.less";
@import "less/mixins.less";
@import "less/variables.less";
```

Here, the @import statement imports code from the file to the main *Less* file. Filenames are written between quotes and followed by a semicolon. Besides the *Less* files, you can also import plain CSS files, which will not be processed for the *Less* directives; this will be explained in more detail in *Chapter 5, Integrating Less in Your Own Projects*.

Now you should open http://localhost/index.html in your browser. You will see a straightforward website layout, which contains a header, content block, side menu, and three-columned footer, as shown in the following screenshot. All the layout items have blue accents. After this, open less/variables.less in your favorite text editor.

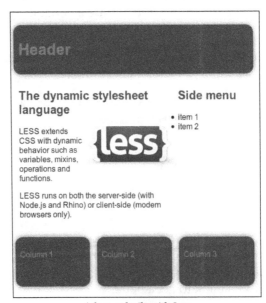

A layout built with *Less*

Curious as you are, I bet you have also opened the other files. Don't be scared by the complexity of the code in them. This code and layout have been used to show the power of widely-used variables that have been defined in a single place. This can be better demonstrated with more realistic and complex examples than by just a few lines of code. Rest assured that all the other code will explain this to you soon. Before you know it, all this code will look very familiar to you.

Firstly, change `darkblue` to `darkgreen` in the `@darkcolor: darkgreen;` line in the `less/variables.less` file, which you opened earlier. After this, watch the results in your browser. Reload your browser if you still haven't used the `#!watch` function.

The layout will now be shown in green. If you weren't convinced earlier, you should be now. In practice, you won't change a complete website using a single line of code, but this example shows what *Less* can do to make your work easier.

Imagine that you have finished your dark-green website's job, and you show it to your boss. "Well done!", he says, but he also tells you, "I know I asked for green, but if you don't mind, I prefer a red website". For now, you smile and simply change `darkgreen` to `darkred` in the `@darkcolor: darkgreen;` line in the `less/variables.less` file.

As you have seen, your HTML is clean and straightforward, with no inline CSS or even class names. There is now a new concern; you will have to name, declare, and save your variables in a smart and proper fashion. When doing this, be consistent and clear as it is of high importance. When organizing your variables, follow the same strategy at all times, using name conventions and comments where the context isn't clear enough. Please keep in mind that someone should be able to take over your work without any further instructions at any moment. To achieve this, you will have to explore the variables at deeper levels.

Naming your variables

You should always give your variables meaningful and descriptive names. Variable names such as `@a1` and `@a2` will get compiled but have not been chosen well. When the number of variables grows or when you have to change something quite deep in the code, you will not know or remember what `@a2` has been used for. You will have to look up its context to find its use in your *Less* files or even worse, inspect your HTML elements to find which CSS rules are applied on it in order to find the *Less* context. In this unfortunate case, you will be back to square one.

Good examples of names include `@nav-tabs-active-link-hover-border-color` and `@dark-color`. These variables are meaningful and descriptive because their names try to describe their function or usage rather than their value. This process of naming will also be called **semantic naming**. So, in this case, `@dark-color` is a better choice than `@red`, and in some cases, you can be more specific by using `@brand-color`. brand. This could describe some house style color of a website, like in the previous case. If the house style color changes from dark red to light green, then `@brand-color: lightgreen;` still makes sense. However, `@dark-color: lightgreen;` or `@red: lightgreen;` just doesn't quite say it.

As you can see, hyphens are used to separate words in variable names. These names are called **hyphenated names**. You should use lower case letters. There aren't any strict rules to use hyphenated names; the so-called **CamelCase** is used and is familiar to many programmers as an acceptable alternative. In CamelCase, you will use something like `@navTabsActiveLinkHoverBorderColor` and `@darkColor`. Both hyphenated and CamelCase names improve readability.

When writing CSS and HTML code, you are using hyphenated two-word terms and lowercase class names, ID's, and font names, among other things. These rules are not always strict, and they are not followed by convention. This book follows this convention when writing *Less* code, and it therefore makes use of hyphenated names.

Whether you prefer CamelCase or hyphenated names doesn't matter greatly. When you have chosen either CamelCase or hyphenated names, it is important to be consistent and use the same way of naming throughout your *Less* files.

When you perform calculations, a hyphenated name may cause some trouble. You will need some extra spacing to solve this. When you declare `@value` minus one, `@value-1` will be read as a single variable instead of `@value -1`.

Using a variable

If your project grows, it will be impossible to add a variable for every CSS property value, so you will have to choose which values should be a variable or which should not. There are no strict rules for this process. You will find some clear guidance to make these choices in the following sections.

You should first try to find property values that are used more than once in your code. Repeated usage is suitable when creating variables. The `@dark-color` variable in the example code is a good example of such a property value.

Second, you can make variables of properties that are used for customization settings. The @basic-width variable in the example code is an example of such a property.

Finally, you should consider creating variables for reusable components. Looking at our example, you could reuse the header in other projects. To make this possible, you should create a new less/header.less file and import this to your main file with the following line of code:

```
@import "less/header.less";
```

Organizing variables

To make components reusable, you can create *Less* files for each component or function and arrange the variables to suit these files. To demonstrate this, split the example code into less/header.less, less/content.less and less/footer.less.

The less/header.less file will now contain the following code:

```
header
{
    background-color: @header-dark-color;
    min-height: @header-height;
    padding: 10px;

    .center-content;
    .border-radius(15px);
    .box-shadow(0 0 10px, 70%);

    h1 {color: @header-light-color;}
}
```

Notice that @dark-color has been renamed as @header-dark-color. Open http://localhost/project.html in your browser and the less/project.less file in the text editor to see all the changes and their effects.

Now, include the less/header.less file in your less/project.less file using @import "header.less"; and create a header section in the less/variablesproject.less file as follows:

```
/* header */
@header-dark-color: @dark-color;
@header-light-color: @light-color;
@header-height: 75px;
```

The `@header-dark-color: @dark-color;` statement assigns the `@dark-color;` value to `@header-dark-color`. After this, you will do the same for `less/content.less` and `less/footer.less`. As you can see, `http://localhost/project.html` still looks the same after your changes.

Now, open `less/variablesproject.less` in your text editor and change the footer section to the following code:

```
/* footer */
@footer-dark-color: darkgreen;
@footer-light-color: lightgreen;
@footer-height: 100px;
@footer-gutter: 10px;
```

In your browser, you will now see the layout with a green footer.

The last declaration wins

In the first chapter, you read about **CSS cascade**, where the last rule said that the value declared last will win if the output of the other rules is equal. *Less* uses the same strategy, where the last declaration of a variable will be used in all the preceding code. In the following code, you will see that the property value is set to 2 in accordance with the last declaration wins rule:

```
@value: 1;
.class{
property: @value;
}
@value: 2;

Compiles into:
.class{

property: 2;

}
```

In fact, *Less* first reads all of your code. When the value of a variable is used, it is only the last-assigned or last-read value that is actually used. The fact that the last declaration wins will only affect the declaration defined in the same scope.

In most programming languages, the scope is defined by a part of the code that the compiler can run independent of the other code. Functions and classes can have their own scope. In *Less*, mixins have their own scope. Mixins will be discussed in more detail later on in this chapter.

The following code shows you that the property value is set to 3 in accordance with the value declared inside the scope of the mixin:

```less
@value: 1;
.mixin(){
  @value: 3;
  property: @value;
}
.class{
  .mixin;
}
@value: 2;Compiles to:
.class{
property: 3;
}
```

The preceding code means you can't change variables during the compilation. This makes these variables theoretical **constants**. Compare this with a definition of the mathematical value of pi in your code, which is always the same. You will define PI only once, where PI = 3.14 will be in your code and will remain constant when your code is run. For this reason, variables should be declared only once.

Redeclaration of variables and the rule that the last declaration wins will be used in the customization of many *Less* projects and code.

To demonstrate redeclaration, create a new less/customized.less file and write the following code into it:

```less
@import "styles.less";
@dark-color: black;
@basic-width: 940px;
```

Reference the customized.less file in the customized.html file as follows:

```html
<link rel="stylesheet/less" type="text/css"
  href="less/customized.less" />
```

Now load the customized.html file in your browser. As you see, you have created a customized version of your layout with only three lines of code!

Variable declaration is not static

Although variables act like constants, their **declaration** is not necessarily unchangeable or static. First, you can assign a value of one variable to another, as shown in the following code:

```
@var2 : 1;
@var1 : @var2;
@var2 : 3;
```

The value of `@var1` is now 3 and not 1. Please understand that you don't need to create some kind of **reference** as the rule that the last declaration wins is applied here. The `@var1` variable will get the value of the last-declared `@var2` variable.

In the example code, you will also find the `@light-color: lighten(@dark-color,40%);` declaration. The `lighten()` function is a so-called built-in function of *Less*. *Chapter 3*, *Nested Rules, Operations, and Built-in Functions*, will cover the built-in functions. The use of the `lighten()` function sets `@light-color` to a calculated color value based on `@dark-color`. You should also pay attention to the last declaration of `@dark-color`, as this is used for color calculation.

Dynamic declaration of variable values gives flexibility, but keep in mind that you should only declare a value once and you can't change it after the declaration.

Lazy loading

Before you switch from variables to mixins, you should first know about **lazy loading**. In computer programming, this means to defer the initialization of an object until the point at which it is needed. Lazy loading is the opposite of eager loading. For *Less*, this means the variables are lazy loaded and do not have to be declared before they are actually used.

It is all very well trying to understand the theoretical aspects, but now, it is time to understand how they work in practice through the following example:

```
.class {
  property: @var;
}
@var: 2;
```

The preceding code gets compiled into the following code:

```
.class {
  property: 2;
}
```

Escaping values

Less is an extension of CSS. This means that *Less* gives an error when it comes across invalid CSS or evaluates a valid CSS during compilation. Some browsers define properties with an invalid CSS. Well-known examples will include something such as `property: ms:somefunction()`. Some of these rules can be replaced by vendor-specific rules. It is important to note that invalid property values won't get compiled in *Less*.

A new function, `calc()`, in CSS3 is a native CSS way of doing simple math as a replacement for a value of any length.

In both cases, *Less* won't give us the right value when we compile or import.

```
@aside-width: 80px;
.content {
width: calc(100% -  @aside-width)
}
```

The preceding code gets compiled into the following code:

```
.content {
  width: calc(20%);
}
```

From the preceding code, `@aside-width: 80px;` is the declaration of a variable with the name `aside-width`. This variable gets a value of 80 pixels. More information on variables will be covered in the following sections. However, more importantly, now the preceding result is wrong (or at least, not as expected) because the `calc()` function should be evaluated during the rendering time. During the render time, the `calc()` function has the ability to mix units, such as percentages and pixels. In the preceding code, `.content` is assigned a width of `100%` of the available space (in other words, all of the available space) minus `80px` (pixels).

Escaping the values will prevent these problems. In *Less*, you can escape values by placing them between quotes (`" "`) preceded by a tilde (`~`). So, in this example, you should write `width: ~"calc(100% -  @{aside-width})"`.

Please note that the accolades are placed in aside-width's variable name, which is called **string interpolation**. In the escaped values, anything between quotes is used as it is, with almost no changes. The only exceptions here are the string **interpolated variables**.

Strings are sequences of characters. In *Less* and CSS, values between quotes are strings. Without escaping, *Less* compiles its strings into CSS strings.

For instance, `width: "calc(100 - 80px)"` doesn't make sense in CSS and neither does `width: calc(100% - @aside-width)` because `@aside-width` has no meaning.

So, with escaping and string interpolation, you can start with the following code snippet:

```
@aside-width: 80px;
.content{
    width: ~"calc(100% - @{aside-width});"
}
```

The preceding code will compile into the following code:

```
.content {
  width: calc(100% - 80px);
}
```

 In the specific case of using the `calc()` function, the *Less* compiler has a **strict-math** option (used since Version 1.4). This is used with `-strict-math=on` in the command line or `strictMath: true` when using JavaScript. When the strict-math option is turned on, the width of `calc(100% - @aside-width);` will get compiled into `width: calc(100% - 80px);`. Notice that there have been many changes to this **strict-math** option during the development of versions 1.6, 1.7, and 2.0.

Mixins

Mixins play an important role in *Less*. You saw mixins in the first chapter when the rounded-corners example was discussed. Mixins take their naming from object-oriented programming. They look like functions in functional programming but in fact act like C macros. Mixins in *Less* allow you to embed all the properties of a class into another class by simply including the class name as one of its properties, as shown in the following code:

```
.mixin(){
  color: red;
      width: 300px;
  padding: 0 5px 10px 5px;
}
p{
.mixin();
}
```

The preceding code will get compiled into the following code:

```
p{
   color: red;
   width: 300px;
   padding: 0 5px 10px 5px;
}
```

In the final CSS code used on the website, every `<p>` paragraph tag will be styled with the properties defined in the `mixin()` function. The advantage will be that you can apply the same mixin on different classes. As seen in the rounded-corners example, you only have to declare the properties once.

Try opening `less/mixins.less` from the available downloadable files of this chapter. In the examples of this book, all mixins are saved to a single file. In this file, you can arrange your mixins based on their functions. Grouping them in a single file prevents us from breaking the code when removing or replacing other functional *Less* files. Your project contains an example in `sidebar.less` and `content.less`, where both files make use of the border-radius mixin. If we now replace `sidebar.less`, you won't break `content.less`. Of course, you also don't want to have the same kind of mixins twice in your code.

The box-sizing mixin in `less/boxsizing.less` will be handled as a specific case. The box-sizing mixin influences all elements, and you want to be able to replace the box-sizing model in its entirety.

The `less/mixins.less` file contains four mixins, which will be discussed in the following sections. The box-shadow and clearfix mixins also have complex structures such as **nesting**, but these mixins will be explained in further detail in the next chapter.

Basic mixins

You have seen the rounded-corners mixin already. A basic mixin looks like a class definition in CSS. Mixins are called inside classes and give these classes their properties.

In the example code in the `less/mixins.less` file, you will find the `.center-content` mixin which sets the value of the `margin` property to `0 auto`. This mixin is used to center align the header, content wrapper, and the footer.

> Note that these center-content mixins are not the one and only solution.
> A general wrapper to center align the header, the content wrapper, and
> the footer at once will also work for this example layout. The name of
> this mixin can also be discussed. When you decide not to center the
> content anymore, the name of this mixin will not make any sense.

Remove the `margin: 0 auto;` property, which in fact centers the content from the
mixin. You should then reload `index.html` in your browser to see the effect.

Parametric mixins

As mentioned earlier, mixins act as functions in functional programming, and so, as
functions, they can be parameterized. A parameter is a value used in combination with
mixins, with the parameter's name used as a reference to its value inside the mixin. The
following code shows you an example of the usage of a parametric mixin:

```
.mixin(@parameter){
  property: @parameter;
}
.class1 {.mixin(10);}
.class2 {.mixin(20);}
```

The preceding code gets compiled to the following code:

```
.class1 {
  property: 10;
}

.class2 {
  property: 20;
}
```

The preceding example shows how parameterization makes mixins very powerful.
They can be used and reused to set properties depending on input values.

Default values

The parameters have an optional default value, which can be defined with
`.mixins(@parameter:defaultvalue);`. To see how this works, you should consider
the border-radius mixin in the `less/mixins.less` file, as seen in the following code:

```
.border-radius(@radius: 10px)
{
  -webkit-border-radius: @radius;
  -moz-border-radius: @radius;
```

```
    border-radius: @radius;
  }
```

Note that the default value here is 10px.

Naming and calling

In this book, mixins have meaningful and descriptive names, and just like variable names, these names are hyphenated. Using meaningful and descriptive names for your mixins makes your code more readable for others and easier to maintain. Parameters and variables both start with an @ sign. The context should make it clear if it is a variable or mixin parameter that is being talked about.

To have a better understanding, consider the following code:

```
@defaulvalue-parameter1 :10;
.mixin(@parameter1: @defaulvalue-parameter1)
{
    property: @parameter1;
}
.class {
  .mixin
}
```

This code can be compiled into the following code:

```
.class{
    property: 10;
}
```

Note that @defaulvalue-parameter1 is a variable here.

The following code also illustrates the scope of a mixin:

```
@defaulvalue-parameter1 :10;
.mixin(@parameter1: @defaulvalue-parameter1){
    property: @parameter1;
}
.class {
  .mixin
}
  @parameter1 : 20;
```

This code can be compiled into the following code:

```
.class{
    property: 10;
}
```

Here, the last declaration of `@parameter1` is outside the scope of the mixin, so the property is still set to 10.

Multiple parameters

Multiple parameters for mixins can be separated by a comma or semicolon. Functional programmers often use a comma as a **separator.** In *Less*, a semicolon is preferred. A comma actually has an ambiguous role here, as they are not only used to separate parameters but also to separate list items in a **csv list**.

The `.mixin(a,b,c,d)` call calls the mixin with four parameters and similarly the `.mixin(a;b;c;d)` call does the same. Now, consider the case where you call the mixin with the `.mixin(a,b,c;d)` call. Only two parameters are used here, and the first parameter is a list of three items. If at least one semicolon is found in the parameter list, then the only separator considered will be the semicolon. The following code shows you the effect of adding an extra semicolon to the parameter list:

```
.mixin(@list){
    property: @list;
}
.class{ mixin(a,b,c,d;);}//see the extra semi-colon!
```

This code can be compiled into the following code:

```
.class{
    property: a, b, c, d;
}
```

Without this extra semicolon, you call a mixin with four parameters. In this case, the compiler throws an error: **RuntimeError: No matching definition was found for .mixin(a, b, c, d)**. What you actually need is a mixin containing `.mixin(@a,@b,@c,@d)`.

In the preceding example, it has been made clear that mixins with the same name are allowed in *Less*. When finding different mixins with the same name, the compiler uses the mixins with the right number of parameters only or throws an error when no matching mixin is found. This form of parametric matching can be compared with **method overloading,** found in various programming languages.

If a mixin call matches more than one mixin, as shown in the following code, then all the matching mixins are used by the compiler:

```
.mixin(@a){
        property-a: @a;
}

.mixin(@b){
```

```
        property-b: @b;
}

class{
      .mixin(value);
}
```

This code gets compiled into the following code:

```
class {
  property-a: value;
  property-b: value;
}
```

More complex mixins for linear gradient backgrounds

You now have enough theoretical knowledge to build more complex mixins. In this example, you will add directive **background gradients** of three colors to the footer columns of our layout.

The end result should look like the following screenshot:

Linear gradient backgrounds built with *Less*

These gradient backgrounds have been chosen because of their complexity and well-documented changes over time. The final result will be a complex mixin, which is definitely not perfect, but improves the result significantly. You can be sure that you will have to change your gradient mixin from time to time because of the drop in support for old browsers, new browsers, changing specifications, and new insights. Refer to `https://developer.mozilla.org/en-US/docs/Web/Guide/CSS/Using_CSS_gradients` for some more examples.

You can't prevent these necessary changes, but you can minimize the time spent on keeping your mixins up to date. *Less* guarantees that all of your background gradients are based on the same mixin defined in a single place.

At a basic level, background gradients in CSS are defined as images. For this reason, they are applied on the **background-image property**.

In this book, gradients are set on the `background-image` property. Other examples (elsewhere and perhaps in other books) will set them on the `background` property. There is no difference in their definitions. CSS defines different properties for backgrounds such as `background-image`, `background-color`, `background-size`, and `background-position`. The `background` property is the shorthand for all of them together. When you define the first value of the `background` property as an image, or gradient in this case, all the other property values are set to their default value.

You start your mixin by making a list of the following **requirements**:

- You want a parameter to set the direction of your gradient, where you will use degrees
- Your gradient will consist of three colors
- After this, you define a list of browsers and the browser version you have to support

Now, you can define the first lines of your mixin as follows:

```
.backgroundgradient(@deg: 0deg; @start-color: green; @between-
  color:yellow; @end-color: red; @between:50%)
{
background-image: linear-gradient(@deg, @start-color, @between-
  color @between, @end-color);
}
```

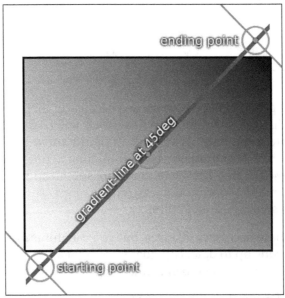

One of the ways to illustrate how the gradient line of 45 degrees works. This was taken from: `http://dev.w3.org/csswg/css-images-3/`, Copyright 2013 W3C, 11 September 2013

The background mixins have five parameters, which are as follows:

- The first parameter describes the direction in degrees. The number of degrees gives the angle between the vertical and the gradient direction. The description of the direction starts at the bottom. At the bottom, the angle is 0 degrees and describes a gradient from bottom to top. Then the angle goes clockwise to 90 degrees point that describes a gradient from left to right, and so on.

- The next three parameters are the three colors of your gradient, which are the default values set for it.

- The fifth and last parameter defines where the middle color has its real value. The percentage here is a percentage of the width of the element that the gradient is applied on. The first and last color has 0 and 100 by default.

Modern browsers, such as IE version 11, Firefox version 16+, Opera version 12.10+, Safari version 7+, and Chrome version 26+, support these background-image properties. For older browsers, vendor-specific rules have to be added. The first problem here is that vendor-specific rules use a different way to define the angle. To compensate for this, you can use a correction of 90 degrees using the following code:

```
.backgroundgradient(@deg: 0deg; @start-color: green; @between-
    color:yellow; @end-color: red; @between:50%){
@old-angel: @deg - 90deg;
-ms-background-image: linear-gradient(@old-angel , @start-color,
    @between-color @between, @end-color);
background-image: linear-gradient(@deg, @start-color, @between-
    color @between, @end-color);
}
```

The `-ms background-image` property is used by IE10, as an older version of IE is unable to support a background image. Alternatively, you can add a filter to support a two-color gradient. There is no support for using this filter in combination with a fallback image, so you will have to choose webkit-based browsers, such as Chrome and Safari, that use `-webkit-linear-gradient`; however, if you have to support older versions of these browsers, you will have to use `-webkit-gradient`. Note that `-webkit-gradient` has an unusual syntax. For example, your final mixin could look like the following code:

```
.backgroundgradient(@degrees: 0deg; @start-color: green; @between-
    color:yellow; @end-color: red; @between:50%){
background-image: -moz-linear-gradient(@degrees, @start-color
    0%, @between-color @between, @end-color 100%);
background: -webkit-gradient(linear, left top, left bottom,
color-stop(0%, @start-color), color-stop(@between,@between-
color), color-stop(100%,@end-color));
```

```
    background-image : -webkit-linear-gradient(@degrees, @start-
      color 0%, @between-color @between, @end-color 100%);
    background-image: -o-linear-gradient(@degrees, @start-color 0%,
      @between-color @between, @end-color 100%);
    background-image: -ms-linear-gradient(@degrees, @start-color 0%,
      @between-color @between, @end-color 100%);
    background-image: linear-gradient((@degrees - 90deg), @start-
      color 0%, @between-color @between, @end-color 100%);
    filter: progid:DXImageTransform.Microsoft.gradient(
      startColorstr='@startcolor',
      endColorstr='@endcolor',GradientType=0 );
}
```

The preceding code shows that even when using *Less*, our code can still be complex. Unless this complexity can support different browsers, you can see the advantage of using *Less*, which allows you to handle this code only once and in a single place.

The code in the preceding example can be found in `directivebackgrounds.html` and `less/directivebackgrounds.less`. If you wonder why you should use a CSS background gradient at all after all of this, then please take a look at `http://lea.verou.me/css3patterns/` and see what is possible.

Special variables – @arguments and @rest

Less defines two special variables. The `@arguments` variable is the first one and contains a list of all the arguments that are passed. The `@arguments` variable exists inside mixins. In *Less*, lists are defined separately with spaces, so you can use `@arguments` for properties that can be set by a list of values. Properties such as `margin` and `padding` accept lists in their shorthand notation, as shown in the following code:

```
.setmargin(@top:10px; @right:10px; @bottom: 10px; @left 10px;){
  margin: @arguments;
}
p{
.setmargin();
}
```

This code can be compiled into the following code:

```
p {
  margin: 10px 10px 10px 10px;
}
```

The second special variable is `@rest`. `@rest...`, which binds all odd arguments after the preceding arguments from the caller to a list. By doing this, `@rest...` gives the opportunity to call a mixin with an endless argument list. Please note that the three ending dots are part of the syntax. The following code shows how `@rest...` binds all the odd parameters after the `@a` variable to the `property2` property:

```
.mixin(@a,@rest...) {
  property1: @a;
            property 2: @rest;
}
element {
    .mixin(1;2;3;4);
}
```

This code will get compiled into the following code:

```
element {

  property1: 1;

  property2: 2 3 4;

}
```

You should also consider using `@rest...` as a csv list. To do this, you can rewrite the `.backgroundgradient` mixin from `less/mixinswithdirectivebackgrounds.less` to the following code:

```
.backgroundgradient(@deg: 0; @colors...) {
    background-repeat: repeat-x;
    background-image: -webkit-linear-gradient(@deg, @colors);
    background-image: -moz-linear-gradient(@deg, @colors);
    background-image: linear-gradient(@deg, @colors);
}
```

Now, the mixin will accept an endless list of colors, and you can use it with the following code:

```
div#content {        .backgroundgradient(0;blue,white,black,pink,purpl
e,yellow,green,or
  ange);
}
```

The following figure shows the result of the code using this background mixin:

Return values

If you are used to functional programming or even know a mathematical function, you expect mixins to have a **return value**. This simply means putting x into it and getting y back. Mixins don't have a return value, but you can mimic this behavior using their scope. A variable defined in a mixin will be copied to the **scope of the caller**, unless the variable has been defined already in the caller's scope. The following example will make this clear:

```
.returnmixin(){
        @par1: 5;
        @par2: 10;
}
.mixin(){
    @par2: 5; // protected for overwriting
        property1: @par1; // copied from returnmixin's scope
        property2: @par2;
        .returnmixin();
}

element{
.mixin();
}
```

This code will get compiled into the following code:

```
element {
   property1: 5;
   property2: 5;
}
```

If you look at the preceding example, you can compare property2: @par2; with a function such as property2 = returnmixin();.

Using the scope to mimic a return value can also be applied on mixins. A mixin defined in another mixin can be used in the scope of the caller. However, these are not protected by the scope like variables are! This process is called **unlocking**. For now, unlocking is outside the scope of this book.

Changing the behavior of a mixin

To make mixins more flexible, it will be useful to influence their output based on their input parameters. *Less* offers different mechanisms in order to do this.

Switches

Imagine that you have a mixin, `color()`; which should set the color property to white or black depending on the context. Set the context with a `@context: light;` declaration and declare two mixins with the same name, as shown in the following code:

```
.color(light)
{
        color: white;
}
.color(dark)
{
        color: black;
}
```

Now you can use the `.color(@context);` mixin in your code which sets the `color` property of your class to white or black, depending on the value declared to `@context`. This may not seem useful now, but it will be useful within your growing project. Take a look at the Bootflat project at `http://www.flathemes.com/`. This project provides color variants of Twitter's Bootstrap. **Twitter's Bootstrap** is a **CSS framework** based on *Less*. Bootflat defines two styles, where one style is based on the improved style of Bootstrap 3.0 and the other style is a Square UI style with the rounded corner removed. This project uses one switch to compile two different styles.

Argument matching

Less allows different mixins with the same name. If there are such mixins, every mixin which matches the caller's parameter list is used. Refer to the following color mixins:

```
.color(@color)
{
  color: @color;
```

```
  }
.color(@color1,@color2)
{
   color: gray;
}
```

With the color mixins defined in the preceding code, `.color(white)` compiles into `color: white;` and `.color(white,black)` will give you `color: gray;`. Note that the `.color(white);` call doesn't match the `.color(@color1,@color2)` mixin, which needs two arguments, and so the compiler did not use it.

Guarded mixins

Mixins of the same name with the same number of arguments are also possible in *Less*. All the matches are used in this case, as shown in the following example:

```
.color(@color){
        color: @color;
        display: block;
}

.color(@color) {
        color: blue;
}
.class{
   .color(white)
}
```

This code will be compiled into the following code:

```
.class{
  color: #ffffff;
  display: block;
  color: blue;
}
```

 Please also note that *Less* converts the named color white to `#ffffff;` here.

Two declarations of `color` don't make sense in this case. *Less* doesn't filter out double declarations unless they are used in the exact same way.

Guards can be used to prevent trouble with double-defined mixins. A guard is defined with a keyword when it is followed by a condition. When the condition is true, a mixin is used. The following example makes things clear:

```
mixin(@a) when (@<1){
    color: white;
}
mixin(@a) when (@>=1){
    color: black;
}
.class {
    mixin(0);
}
.class2 {
    mixin(1);
}
```

This code will be compiled to the following code:

```
.class {
  color: white;
}
.class2 {
  color: black;
}
```

Guards can be used as an *if* statement in programming. The comparison operators such as >, >=, =, =<, and < can be used. One or more conditions can be combined in the same way when separated with commas, which evaluates as true if one of them is true.

The keyword and can be used to evaluate as true only when both conditions are true, for instance, when @a>1 and @<5. And finally, a condition can be negated with the keyword not, for instance, when (not a = red).

If you have used CSS media queries earlier, then you must realize that guards act in the very same way that a media query does in CSS.

Finally, guard conditions can also contain built-in functions. These functions will be discussed in the next chapter and act on all defined variables when they are not part of the argument list. The built-in functions of the guard conditions can be seen in the following code:

```
@style: light;
.mixin(@color) when is_color(@color) and (@style = light) {
  color: pink;
}
.class() {
  mixin(red);
}
```

This code can be compiled into the following code:

```
.class {
  color: pink;
}
```

In the case of `@style: dark;` or `mixin(1);`, there was no match.

Using guards and argument matching to construct loops

When *Less* doesn't find a **matching mixin**, it goes to the next evaluation and doesn't break. This can be used in combination with guards and argument matching to construct loops. To show this, imagine 10 **classes**, each containing a numbered background image. The `.class1` class has the `background-image` property value set to `background-1.png`, the `.class2` class has set the value of the `background-image` property to `background-2.png`, and so on, as seen in the following code:

```
.setbackground(@number) when (@number>0){
  .setbackground( @number - 1 );
  .class@{number} { background-image: ~"url (backgroundimage-
    @{number}.png)"; }
}
.setbackground(10);
```

This code can be compiled into the following code:

```
.class1 {
  background-image: url(backgroundimage-1.png);
}
.class2 {
  background-image: url(backgroundimage-2.png);
}
```

```
...
.class10 {
  background-image: url(backgroundimage-10.png);
}
```

The last mixin perhaps looks complex when you see it first, but if you try to evaluate the mixin yourself, you will see that it actually contains a lot of stuff you have learned before.

In the preceding code, the `setbackground` mixin calls itself. Programmers will call this a **recursion**. What happens here?

The `.setbackground(10);` call matches the `.setbackground(@number)` mixin when `@number>0`, so please make use of this. The first evaluation of `.setbackground( @number - 1 );` also matches the mixin. This means that the compiler runs the mixin again. This will repeat until `@number -1` is `0`; no matches can be found anymore. Now the compiler will read ahead of where it stopped in order to use the mixin.

The last stop was at `@number = 1`, so it evaluates the `.class@{number} { background-image: ~"url(backgroundimage-@{number}.png)"; }` declaration for the `@numer = 1` condition. When it stopped before, it was at `@number = 2`. So, it evaluates the `.class@{number} { background-image: ~"url(backgroundimage-@ {number}.png)"; }` declaration for the `@numer = 2` condition, and so on. When we are back at `@numer = 10`, all the code has been compiled. So, the compiler stops.

Besides guards and argument matching, the preceding example also contains an interpolated property in the `.class@{number}` class declaration, as well as an example string interpolation with escaping when declaring the `~"url(backgroundimage-@{number}.png)";` code. Mixins also show the need to use an additional space when performing calculations. So, `@number - 1` won't be evaluated as one `@number-1` variable.

The !important keyword

The chapter ends with a note on the `!important` keyword in *Less*. Using `!important` in a declaration gives the declaration the highest precedence when two or more selectors match the same element. The `!important` keyword overrules inline styles, as shown in the following code:

```
<style>
p{color:green !important;}
</style>
<p style="color:red;">green</p>
```

The preceding code will show the text in green. As the example shows you, you can use !important to change the styles, which you cannot edit, of the source with inline CSS. It can also be used to make sure a style is always applied. Nevertheless, please use !important with care, as the only way to overrule !important is to use another !important. Any incorrect or unnecessary use of !important in *Less* will make your code messy and difficult to maintain.

In *Less*, you can not only use !important for properties, but you can also use it with mixins. When !important is set for a certain mixin, all the properties of this mixin will be declared with the !important keyword. This can be seen in the following code:

```
.mixin(){property1: 1;property2: 2;
}
.class{
.mixin() !important;
}
```

This code will be compiled into the following code:

```
.class{
  property1: 1 !important;
  property2: 2 !important;
}
```

Summary

In this chapter, you learned about variables and mixins. You have seen how defining variables and mixins at a single place will reduce your code and make it easy to maintain.

In the next chapter, you will learn more about mixins and how to nest and extend them. You will also read about the built-in functions of *Less*. Built-in functions can be used to manipulate values in mixins and other parts of your code.

3
Nested Rules, Operations, and Built-in Functions

In this chapter, you will learn how *Less* helps you organize your CSS selectors more intuitively, makes inheritance clear, and makes your style sheets shorter. You will also learn about operations and built-in functions. Operations let you add, subtract, divide, and multiply property values and colors. They also give you the power to create complex relationships between properties. You will also learn how to set variables or guards using the built-in functions in your *Less* code.

This chapter will cover the following topics:

- Nesting CSS rules
- Using operations
- Using built-in functions in you code
- Using built-in functions in your mixins

The navigation structure

With the examples in this chapter, you will extend the layout from *Chapter 2, Using Variables and Mixins* step by step with a navigation structure. You will build this navigation structure by styling an HTML list with *Less*. This navigation structure forms a menu in the sidebar of the layout.

The final result will look like the following screenshot:

The final navigation menu built using *Less*

Nested rules

You will use the layout example from *Chapter 2, Using Variables and Mixins,* to study *nesting of rules* in more detail.

To do this, you must first open `http://localhost/index.html` in your browser and then open `less/sidebar.less` in your text editor.

Anchors are added to the menu items. This means that the HTML code of the side menu now looks like the following code:

```
<aside id="sidemenu">
  <h2>Side menu</h2>
  <ul>
      <li><a href="page1.html">item 1</a></li>
      <li><a href="page2.html">item 1</a></li>
  </ul>
</aside>
```

You need a selector for each rule to style the different elements in CSS as can be seen in the following code:

```
#sidebar h2{
  color: black;
  font-size: 16px;
}
#sidebar ul li a{
```

```
      text-decoration: none;
      color: green;
   }
```

As you can see, both the `ul` (including the `li` element and the `a` anchor) element and the `h2` element are the children of the `aside` element with the `#sidemenu` ID. CSS doesn't reflect this relationship because it is currently in the format as shown in the preceding code. *Less* will help you to reflect this relationship in your code. In *Less*, you can write the following code:

```
#sidebar{
   h2{
      color: black;
      font-size: 16px;
   }
   ul{
      li{
         a{
            text-decoration: none;
            color: green;
         }
      }
   }
}
```

The preceding code will compile straight into the following CSS syntax:

```
#sidebar h2 {
   color: black;
   font-size: 16px;
}
#sidebar ul li a {
   text-decoration: none;
   color: green;
}
```

The resulting CSS of your compiled *Less* code is exactly the same as your original CSS code. In *Less*, you refer to the `#sidemenu` ID only once, and due to the nesting of `h2` and `ul` inside `#sidemenu`, your code structure is intuitive and reflecting the **DOM structure** of your HTML code.

To keep your code clean, a new `less/sidebar.less` file has been created. It contains the preceding *Less* code. Of course, this file should also be imported into `less/styles.less` using the following line of code:

```
@import "sidebar.less";
```

Please also note that the sidebar is wrapped in a semantic HTML5 `aside` element instead of a `div` element. Although this is more semantic, you will find that your sidebar has floated to the left after you made these changes. To fix this, open `less/content.less` in your text editor. By studying the nesting of the CSS selectors in the *Less* code, you will find `aside float:right;` nested in the `.wrapper` container. If you move this `aside` rule inside the `#content` container, the syntax should look like the following code:

```
#content {
  //two third of @basic-width
  width:(@basic-width * 2 / 3);
  float:left;
  min-height:200px;
  aside {
    float:right;
  }
}
```

In the `less/content.less` file, you will also find the line `h2 { color: @content-dark-color; }`, which is in contrast to what you will see in the `aside` element. The `h2` rule will still be overwritten by `#sidebar h2{ color: black; }`. The final rule contains a `#sidebar` selector and so it has a higher **CSS specificity**, as explained in the first chapter.

Inspect the *Less* files, such as `less/header.less`, again and keep these brand new insights about nesting of CSS selectors in mind. You will see that nesting is already used frequently. For example, in `less/header.less`, the properties of the `h1` element are set by nesting.

A proper inspection of these files will also show you how mixins can be nested in classes and other mixins.

Mixins and classes

The name of a mixin should always end with parentheses; otherwise, it is a normal **class**. Both mixins and classes can be nested in *Less*. Consider the difference in the following example *Less* code:

```
.class-1{
  property-1: a;
}
.class-2{
  .class-1;
  property-2: b;
}
```

This code gets compiled into the following code:

```
.class-1 {
  property-1: a;
}
.class-2 {
  property-1: a;
  property-2: b;
}
```

You can see how the properties of .class-1 are copied into .class-2 in the compiled CSS. When you add parentheses after .class-1 in *Less* and make it a mixin, you should now consider the following code:

```
.mixin(){
  property-1: a;
}
.class-2{
  .mixin;
  property-2: b;
}
```

This code will get compiled into the following CSS code:

```
.class-2 {
  property-1: a;
  property-2: b;
}
```

Let's go back to the example of the side navigation menu. When your menu is ready, you will find that the "navigating" text inside the h2 heading element makes no sense. Unless you are visually impaired and use a screen reader, you can easily see the side menu is intended as navigation for the website. So, you can hide this heading but should keep it visible for **screen readers**. Setting display:none will hide the element from screen readers, while visibility:hidden will also hide the element but still takes space and so can mess up our design. Setting the clip property will help in this situation. You can find more details by visiting http://a11yproject.com/posts/how-to-hide-content/.

Based on the rule of precedence, you can write the following class using *Less*:

```
.screenreaders-only {
  clip: rect(1px, 1px, 1px, 1px);
  position: absolute;
  border:0;
}
```

Add the preceding class to `less/boxsizing.less` and rename this file as `less/basics.less`. Also, please don't forget to rename the import statement in `less/styles.less`. Now you can use the following *Less* code to hide the h2 heading element in the sidebar menu:

```
#sidebar{
  h2{
    color: black;
    font-size: 16px;
    .screenreaders-only;
  }
}
```

After performing these steps and compiling the *Less* code into the CSS code, the sidebar navigation will now look like the following screenshot:

- item 1
- item 2
- item 3
- item 4
- item 5
- item 6

A styled navigation menu with hidden heading text

As `.screenreaders-only` is a class and not a mixin, and classes are compiled to your final CSS, not only can you use the `.screenreaders-only` class to add its properties to other classes in *Less*, but you can also use the class in your HTML directly, as shown in the following line of code:

```
<div class="screenreaders-only">Only readable for screen
    readers</div>
```

When working with *Less*, you will often have to choose between specific compiled *Less* classes based on your project's HTML structure and a more generic solution that will be applied with a class inside your HTML code. Unfortunately, in these cases, there is no single solution. In general, DOM-specific code will generate more CSS code but will also keep your HTML clean and give you the opportunity to generate more semantic HTML code. Reusing your *Less* code won't always be simple for this option.

Compiling your *Less* syntax as classes and using them in your HTML will make your code more reusable. On the other hand, it will mess up your HTML due to these classes. Also, the relationship between the CSS effects and HTML structure becomes less strict. This makes it more difficult to maintain or change.

Variables

In `less/variables.less`, you should define a section for your sidebar, as shown in the following code:

```
/* side bar */
@header-color: black;
@header-font-size: 16px;
/* menu */
@menu-background-color: white;
@menu-font-color: green;
@menu-hover-background-color: darkgreen;
@menu-hover-font-color: white;
@menu-active-background-color: lightgreen;
@menu-active-font-color: white;
```

With the preceding variables, the *Less* code in `less/sidebar.less` will now look like the following code:

```
#sidebar{
  h2{
    color: @header-color;
    font-size: @header-font-size;
    .screenreaders-only;
  }
  ul{
    li{
      a{
        text-decoration: none;
        color: @menu-font-color;
        background-color: @menu-background-color;
        }
      }
    }
  }
}
```

Classes and namespaces

Before finishing the menu, the *Less* code used to style the menu will be changed to a class first. The points to consider here have already been discussed. A navigation is a general structure that can be used in many projects. In the class structure, it can be used to style any HTML list.

Please create a new file for `less/nav.less` and write the following code into it:

```less
.nav{
  li{
    a{
      text-decoration: none;
      color: @menu-font-color;
      background-color: @menu-background-color;
      }
    }
}
```

Now you can turn every HTML list (`ul` or `ol`) in our HTML document into a navigation structure just by adding the `.nav` class to it. This can be done using the following line of code:

```html
<ul class="nav">
```

Please notice that with this *Less* code, lists can't be nested, and the items on the list should contain anchors (links). These requirements make it seem clear that this code can easily be (re)used in your other projects. *Less* also offers the possibility of defining **namespaces**. Namespaces can make your code more portable and are defined in the same way as CSS ID selectors. Namespaces start with a #, as shown in the following code:

```less
#lessnamespace {
  .nav {
    //code from  less/nav.less here
  }
}
```

The `#lessnamespace` namespace can now be used as an example, as shown in the following code:

```less
#sidebar {
  ul{
    #lessnamespace > .nav;
  }
}
```

In fact, a namespace doesn't differ from an ID selector. The #lessnamespace namespace can also be used directly in your HTML code, although this is not useful in most cases, as shown in the following code:

```
<div id="lessnamespace">
  <ul class="nav">
    ...
  </ul>
</div>
```

HTML requires every ID to be defined only once, so you can't use the preceding HTML code more than once in your HTML document unless you append the ID to the body. Nevertheless, the preceding code shows that even specifically written *Less* code for a custom HTML DOM structure can be reused in other projects.

In the #lessnamespace namespace, as defined earlier, .nav is a class that makes direct usage possible. When .nav is changed to a mixin, it can only be reused in *Less*, as shown in the following code:

```
#namespace {
  .nav(){
    li{
      width:100%;
    }
  }
}
#sidebar {
  ul{
    #namespace > .nav;
  }
}
```

This code will get compiled straight into the following code:

```
#sidebar ul li {
  width: 100%;
}
```

Operating on numbers, colors, and variables

Less has support for the basic arithmetic operations: addition (+), subtraction (-), multiplication (*), and division (/). In the strict-math mode, operations should be placed between parentheses. You can apply an operation on variables, values, and numbers. These will help you make relationships between variables.

Open `less/footer.less` to immediately see the operation that you used, as in the following code, and its benefits:

```
footer {
  div {
     float: left;
    width: ((@basic-width / 3 ) - @footer-gutter);
    }
}
```

In the preceding code, the / sign (division) has been used to give the footer columns one-third of the available width (as set by `@basic-width`). Using operations in your code feels so natural that you may not have even realized you have been using them until now. *Less* uses normal **order precedence**, where you can add extra parentheses to explicitly set precedence and avoid confusion. For instance, in *Less*, 3 + 3 * 3 gives 12. So, (3 + 3) * 3 equals 18, as shown in the following code:

```
.mixin(){
  property1: (3 + 3 * 3);
  property2: ((3 + 3) * 3);
}
.class {
.mixin;
}
```

This code will get compiled into the following code:

```
.class {
  property1: 12;
  property2: 18;
}
```

Less operations can also be used for color manipulation and operations can be applied on values and colors with different units, as shown in the following code:

```
@color: yellow;
.mixin(){
  property1: (100px * 4);
```

```
    property2:  (6% * 1px);
    property3:  (#ffffff - #111111);
    property4:  (@color / 10%)
  }
  .class {
  .mixin;
  }
```

This code will get compiled into the following code:

```
  .class {
    property1: 400px;
    property2: 6%;
    property3: #eeeeee;
    property4: #1a1a00;
  }
```

The & symbol

The & symbol plays a special and important role in *Less*. It refers to the parent of the current selector and you can use it to reverse the order of nesting and to extend or merge classes. You will see that the following example will tell you more than what can be expressed in a thousand words:

```
  .class1
  {
    .class2{
      property: 5;
    }
  }

  .class1
  {
    .class2 & {
      property: 5;
    }
  }
```

This code will compile into the following code:

```
  .class1 .class2 {
    property: 5;
  }
  .class2 .class1 {
    property: 5;
  }
```

You can see that `.class2` becomes the parent of `.class1` when you use the `&` symbol after it. The `&` symbol can also be used in order to reference nesting that is outside the mixin.

The `&` symbol can also be used to nest and append **pseudo classes** to a class. Later on, you will see that you can use it to append classes too. A simple example of this will be adding a `:hover` pseudo class triggered by a mouse hover to a link, as shown in the following code:

```
.hyperlink{
  color: blue;
  &:hover {
    color: red;
  }
}
```

This code can be compiled into the following code:

```
.hyperlink {
  color: blue;
}
.hyperlink:hover {
  color: red;
}
```

Now, open `less/mixins.less` in your text editor and find the **clearfix mixin**. The clearfix mixin uses the `&` symbol to append the `:hover`, `:after`, and `:before` pseudo classes to your elements, as shown in the following code:

```
.clearfix() {
  &:before,
  &:after {
    content: " "; /* 1 */
    display: table; /* 2 */
  }
  &:after {
    clear: both;
  }
}
```

With this new knowledge about the `&` symbol, it will now be easy for you to understand how to extend your example navigation menu with the `:hover` and `:active` (`.active`) states, and the following code shows you how your extended code will look:

```
.nav {
    li {
      a {
```

```
        text-decoration: none;
        color: @menu-font-color;
        &:hover {
          color:@menu-hover-font-color;
          background-color:@menu-hover-background-color;
        }
      width:100%;
      display: block;
      padding: 10px 0 10px 10px;
      border: 1px solid @menu-border-color;
      margin-top: -1px;// prevent double border
    }
    &.active {
      a {
        color:@menu-active-font-color;
        background-color:@menu-active-background-color;
      }
    }
    &:first-child a {
      border-radius: 15px 15px 0 0;
    }
    &:last-child a{
      border-radius: 0 0 15px 15px;
    }

  }

  list-style: none outside none;
  padding:0;
}
```

Open `http://localhost/indexnav.html` in your browser to inspect the results of the preceding syntax.

The `extend` pseudo-class is a *Less* pseudo-class and uses the same syntax as a CSS pseudo-class. The `extend` pseudo-class adds the selector to the **extended selector list**. Adding the selector to the selector list of a different class gives the selector the same properties as the extended class. Remember the `.hyperlink` class in a previous example? If you extend this class, then both classes will have the same properties:

```
.hyperlink{
  color: blue;
  &:hover {
    color: red;
  }
}
        .other-hyperlink:extend(.hyperlink){};
```

This code will get compiled into the following code:

```
.hyperlink,
.other-hyperlink {
    color: blue;
}
.hyperlink:hover {
    color: red;
}
```

Notice that the nested `:hover` pseudo class is not covered in `.other-hyperlink`. To extend a class including the nested elements of the extended style, you will have to add the `all` keyword, as shown in the following code:

```
.other-hyperlink:extend(.hyperlink all){};
```

This code now gets compiled into the following code:

```
.hyperlink,

.other-hyperlink {

    color: blue;

}

.hyperlink:hover,

.other-hyperlink:hover {

    color: red;

}
```

In cases where you nest the `:extend` statement, you have to use the `&` symbol as a reference, as shown in the following code:

```
.other-hyperlink{
    &:extend(.hyperlink);
};
```

In spite of the fact that the `extend` syntax mimics the syntax of the pseudo class, both of them can be combined as long as `:extend` is added at the end of the selector, as shown in the following code:

```
.other-hyperlink:hover:extend(.hyperlink){};
```

Property merging

Property merging is useful if properties accept a **Comma Separated Value (CSV)**. You will find this type of property mostly in CSS3, where borders, backgrounds, and transitions accept a CSV list. However, you will also find that the old-school `font-family` parameter accepts a list of font names that are separated by commas. Properties are merged by adding a plus sign (+) after their names, as shown in the following code:

```
.alternative-font()
{
  font-family+: Georgia,Serif;
}
.font()
{
  font-family+: Arial;
  .alternative-font;
}
body {
.font;
}
```

This code will get compiled into the following code:

```
body {
  font-family: Arial, Georgia,Serif;
}
```

Built-in functions

Less supports many handy **built-in functions**. A built-in function can be used to manipulate *Less* values inside mixins and set the variables' values. Last but not least, they can also be used in **guard expressions**. You will find the complete list of functions by visiting `http://lesscss.org/functions/`.

In this chapter, you won't find them all, but you will learn how to use functions from all different groups. Functions can be grouped based on their input and output types, where these types are mathematical functions, color functions, list functions, string functions, and type functions. There is also a small number of functions that can't be grouped using the preceding classification.

JavaScript

Less functions map native **JavaScript functions** and code in the first place because of the fact that *Less* has been written in JavaScript. Currently, JavaScript expressions can still be evaluated as values inside *Less* code, but this ability may be removed in future versions. JavaScript code should be wrapped between back quotes when used in your *Less* code, as shown in the following code:

```
@max: ~"`Math.max(10,100)+'px'`";
p {
  width: @max;
}
```

This *Less* code, which includes JavaScript code, will compile into the following CSS code:

```
p {

  width: 100px;

}
```

Even though it is possible, try to avoid using JavaScript in your code. **Less compilers** written in other languages can't evaluate this code, so your code is not portable and is more difficult to maintain.

If there is no built-in *Less* function available for your purpose, try to write the equivalent of what you need in *Less* code. Since Version 1.6, there is a max() function, and previously, you could use the following code:

```
.max(@a,@b) when (@a>=@b){@max:@a;}
.max(@a,@b) when (@b>@a){@max:@b;}
```

In particular, watch out when using the JavaScript environment in your *Less* code. Also, values such as document.body.height make no sense in your compiled and stateless CSS.

List functions

Extract() and length() are functions to get the values and the length of a CSV list. Together, these functions can be used to **iterate** as arrays over a CSV list.

Remember the loop used to set background images in *Chapter 2, Using Variables and Mixins*? Here, you will use the same technique to add icons before the links in the sidebar navigation.

This example uses icons from Font Awesome. Font Awesome is an iconic font that uses scalable vector icons which can be manipulated by CSS. Icons can be scaled or colored easily with CSS; also, loading the font requires only one HTTP request for all icons. Please refer to http://fontawesome.io/ for more information.

To use Font Awesome, reference its source first by adding the following line of code to the head section of your HTML document:

```
<link href="//netdna.bootstrapcdn.com/font-awesome/4.0.3/css/font-
    awesome.css" rel="stylesheet">
```

 Font Awesome and other iconic fonts can also be integrated and compiled into your project using *Less*. You will learn how to do this in *Chapter 4, Avoid Reinventing the Wheel*.

In your HTML, you can now use the following line of code:

```
<i class="fa fa-camera-retro"></i> fa-camera-retro
```

Icons are added with the CSS :before pseudo class, so the preceding HTML code can also be styled without a class by using the following *Less* code:

```
i:before {
  font-family:'FontAwesome';
  content:"\f083";
}
```

 A list of Font Awesome icons and their CSS content values can be found by visiting http://astronautweb.co/ snippet/font-awesome/.

With this information about iconic fonts, you can construct a loop that adds icons to the list items of your navigation, as shown in the following code:

```
@icons: "\f007","\f004","\f108","\f112","\f072","\f17c";
.add-icons-to-list(@i) when (@i > 0) {
  .add-icons-to-list((@i - 1));
  @icon_: e(extract(@icons, @i));
  li:nth-child(@{i}):before {
    font-family:'FontAwesome';
    content: "@{icon_}\00a0";
  }
}
.add-icons-to-list(length(@icons));
```

In the `@icon_: e(extract(@icons, @i));` line, `e()` is a **string function**, and this function is the equivalent of escaping using `~""`. Please also note that in the `content: "@{icon_}\00a0";` statement, `\00a0` only adds an extra space that separates the icon from the link.

The icons in the `@icons` CSV list are randomly chosen. The recursive calling of the `add-icons-to-list()` mixin starts with the `.add-icons-to-list(length(@icons));` call, where `length(@icons)` returns the number of items in `@icons`.

The *Less* code of the loop which adds icons to the list items should be added into `less/navicons.less`. After adding the code, open `http://localhost/indexnavicons.html` to see the results, which should look like the following screenshot:

Iconized hyperlinks built with Less and Font Awesome

The icon list in the preceding screenshot serves only for demonstration purposes, where, in fact, the icons are not even related to the hyperlinks. The absence of this relationship makes it difficult to find a use case at all. However, with your creative minds, I bet you can find one. Remember that CSS is used only for presentation and cannot modify HTML, so you can't set the links themselves using *Less*. However, creating a relationship between the hyperlinks and icons that already exist is possible, as shown in the following code:

```
#content a[href*="linux"]:before {
  font-family:'FontAwesome';
  content: "\f17c\00a0";
}
```

Here, a `[href*="linux"]` is a selector for all anchors with the word `linux` in their `href` attribute. After adding the preceding code to `less/styles.less`, you can view the results at `http://localhost/index.html`.

Using color functions

Less color functions can be split into functions for **color definition, blending, operations**, and **channel manipulation**.

Colors are defined in **color channels.** An RGB color has three channels: red, green, and blue. CSS2 used this RGB definition to declare colors, and CSS3 adds new definitions for color declaration. These new definitions, such as HSL and HSV, are nothing more than transformations of RGB values. The CSS3 color setting methods should be more intuitive and user friendly. For instance, HSL defines colors in three channels, which are hue, saturation, and lightness in this case. *Less* has built-in functions for channel manipulation of different types of color definitions. *Less* also supports different types of color definitions. Since CSS3, you can declare color values as hexadecimal colors, RGB colors, RGBA colors (RGB colors with an additional alpha channel that sets the opacity), HSL colors, and HSLA colors (HSL colors with an additional alpha channel that also sets the opacity). Of course, you are allowed to use the predefined cross-browser color names.

The compiled color values of *Less*'s color definitions are not always defined as a hexadecimal color in CSS code; if possible, the output of a color definition matches the CSS values, as shown in the following code:

```
.selector {

  color1: rgb(32,143,60);

  color2: rgba(32,143,60,50%);

  color3: hsl(90, 100%, 50%);

}
```

The preceding *Less* code becomes the following CSS code after compilation:

```
.selector {

  color1: #208f3c;

  color2: rgba(32, 143, 60, 0.5);

  color3: #80ff00;

}
```

Colors are a basic part of the design and styling of your website. Color functions can help you design your **color palettes** and make them dynamic. They will be used, for instance, to give elements a border color that is darker than the background color or to give elements contrasting colors that are based on a single input color.

The darken() and lighten() functions

The darken() and lighten() functions are two color functions that can be used to obtain a darker or lighter variant of the input color. You have seen how these functions have been used in the example layout from *Chapter 2, Using Variables and Mixins*. Now you can apply these functions on the website navigation menu you have built previously.

Please open less/variablesnav.less in your text editor and define your menu variables that are dependent on the main @menucolor parameter as follows:

```
@menucolor: green;
@menu-background-color: white;
@menu-font-color: @menucolor;
@menu-border-color: darken(@menucolor,10%);
@menu-hover-background-color: darken(@menucolor,10%);
@menu-hover-font-color: white;
@menu-active-background-color: lighten(@menucolor,10%);
@menu-active-font-color: white;
```

After doing this, check your changes by opening http://localhost/indexnav. html in your browser. Now you can modify the look of your navigation by only changing the color defined by the @menucolor variable. You will also find that setting @menucolor to a light color, such as pink or yellow, makes your fonts unreadable due to the **contrast** between the background color and the font color not being high enough. High contrast plays an important role in web design. Designs with high contrast help you meet **accessibility** standards. High contrast not only helps visibly disabled or color blind people, it also influences those with normal vision, as humans are naturally in favor of high contrast color designs. This favor plays a role in the first impression of your website.

Calculating the right amount of contrast is not always easy. Also, in this case, you don't want to have to change all your font colors after changing the basic color. The contrast() function of *Less* will help you to choose a color that can easily be seen against a colored background. In accordance with WCAG 2.0 (http://www.w3.org/ TR/2008/REC-WCAG20-20081211/#relativeluminancedef), this function compares the **luma** value and not the lightness of the colors. The luma() function itself is also a built-in color function.

The `contrast()` function accepts four parameters. The first parameter defines the color to be compared against; this is the background color in this particular case. The second and third parameters define the dark and light color, which are black and white by default. The fourth and last parameter sets a threshold. This threshold has been set to 43 percent by default and defines the luma (perceptual brightness). Colors above the threshold are considered as light, and `contrast()` returns the dark color that is already defined in the second parameter for these light colors.

Now, reopen `less/variablesnav.less` and change the navigating font colors according to the following code:

```
@menucolor: green;
@menu-background-color: white;
@menu-font-color: contrast(@menucolor);
@menu-border-color: darken(@menucolor,10%);
@menu-hover-background-color: darken(@menucolor,10%);
@menu-hover-font-color: contrast(@menu-hover-background-color);
@menu-active-background-color: lighten(@menucolor,10%);
@menu-active-font-color: contrast(@menu-active-background-color);
```

To see more effects, change the `@menucolor` variable to different colors such as `yellow`, `pink`, `darkgreen`, or `black` and observe the change by opening `http://localhost/indexnav.html`. Keep in mind that the lightest color is white and the darkest is black, so `darken(black,10%);` or `lighten(white,10%);` won't have any effect.

Color manipulation

As mentioned earlier, *Less* provides you with many functions to manipulate colors. This book is not about **color theory**, so it handles only some examples of color manipulation. You can find more information about color theory by visiting `http://www.packtpub.com/article/introduction-color-theory-lighting-basics-blender`.

Color operations

With the `darken()`, `lighten()`, and `contrast()` functions, you have become acquainted with some of the color operations. Other operations include `saturate()`, `desaturate()`, `fadein()`, `fadeout()`, `fade()`, `spin()`, `mix()`, and `grayscale()`.

The functions mentioned earlier accept one or more color values, with the percentage as an input parameter, and return a color. Please note that the color ranges from white to black and does not wrap around. So, you can't, as mentioned earlier, darken the color black so that it becomes white.

If color definitions contain percentages, then the operations change them with the absolute percentage of the input parameter. So, `darken(hsl(90, 80%, 50%), 20%)` becomes `#4d8a0f;` which equals `hsl(90, 80%,30%)` and *not* `hsl(90, 80%,10%)`. Of course, you will see the same effect as you manipulate the second channel, which defines saturation. For instance, `desaturate(hsl(45, 65%, 40%), 50%)` compiles into `#756e57;`, which equals `hsl(45, 15%, 40%)`.

The `mix()` function is the last example of color operations. The other functions are left for you as exercises.

```
@color: mix(blue, yellow, 50%);
.class {
color: @color;
}
```

This will again become the following:

```
.class {
  color: #808080;
}
```

This mixture will also be shown in the following image :

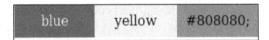

How a mixture of blue and yellow is presented using `mix(blue, yellow, 50%)`

Color blending with Less

The color blending functions calculate a new color based on two input colors, where functions apply basic operations such as subtraction on the color channels of the input colors. Available functions, also called blend modes, include `multiply()`, `screen()`, `overlay()`, `softlight()`, `hardlight()`, `difference()`, `exclusion()`, `average()`, and `negation()`. Users of layered image editors such as Photoshop or GIMP will recognize these functions.

The `difference()` function subtracts the second color from the first color on a channel-by-channel basis, as shown in the following code:

```
@color: difference(orange, red, 50%);
.class {
color: @color;
}
```

The preceding code will become the following code:

```
.class {
  color:   #00a500;
}
```

The following figure shows how a mixture of orange and red would appear:

How a mixture of orange and red will appear using difference(orange, red, 50%)

Type functions

Type functions evaluate the type of the input value and return as true if the type matches the function. The functions that are available are isnumber(), isstring(), iscolor(), iskeyword(), isurl(), ispixel(), isem(), ispercentage(), and isunit(). Some example functions are shown in the following code:

```
isnumber("string"); // false
isnumber(1234); // true
isnumber(56px); // true
iscolor(#ff0); // true
iscolor(blue); // true
iscolor("string"); // false
ispixel(1234); // false
ispixel(56px); // true
```

Type functions are useful in defining guards. Please consider the following syntax:

```
.mixin() when isprecentage(@value) {
  width: 25%;
}
.mixin() when ispixel(@value) {
  width: (@value / 4 );
}
```

The default() function is another built-in function that is not grouped in a function class. The default() function can be used inside a guard and returns as true when none of the other mixins match the caller. You can add a default mixin to the preceding mixins, as shown in the following code:

```
.mixin() when ispercentage(@value) {
  width: 25%;
}
```

```
.mixin() when ispixel(@value) {
  width: (@value / 4 );
}
.mixin() when (default()) {
  display: none;
}
```

The box-shadow mixin

With all that you have learned about *Less*, you now can understand, build, and evaluate any complex *Less* code. To prove this, please open `less/mixins.less` and take a look at the box-shadow mixin (originally published on `lesscss.org`), which looks like the following code:

```
.box-shadow(@style, @c) when (iscolor(@c)) {
  -webkit-box-shadow: @style @c;
  -moz-box-shadow:    @style @c;
  box-shadow:         @style @c;
}
.box-shadow(@style, @alpha: 50%) when (isnumber(@alpha)) {
  .box-shadow(@style, rgba(0, 0, 0, @alpha));
}
```

To fully understand these mixins, you will have to know the basics of **box-shadow** in CSS3. The box-shadow properties accept a CSV list of shadows. A shadow consists of a list of two to four length values and a color. The first two length values describe the vertical and horizontal offsets related to the center of the box. These values are required but can be set to 0 to get an equal-size shadow around the box. The final values are optional and set the blur radius and the spread radius, respectively. The blur and spread radii are both 0 by default and give a sharp shadow, where the spread radius equals the blur radius.

Now you should be able to evaluate the mixin. You will see that the mixins form a guard. Both mixins accept two parameters. The first parameter is the length vector, which is described earlier; the second is a color or a percentage. If you recall that the `isnumber(40%)` call evaluates as `true` despite the ending percent sign. Calling `rgba(0, 0, 0, @alpha)` will give shades of gray depending on the value of `@alpha`. If you define the second parameter as a color, such as `blue` or `#0000ff#`, the `iscolor(@c)` guard will evaluate as `true`, and the first mixin will be compiled using your defined color.

Summary

In this chapter, you built a navigation menu with *Less*. The navigation contains, amongst other things, hovers, contrast colors, and icons that can all be set with a few basic settings. You have learned how to use nesting rules, mixins, and built-in functions in *Less*. At the end of the chapter, you have understood and used complex *Less* code. All this newly acquired knowledge will be very useful in the next chapter. In the next chapter, you will learn how to find and build reusable *Less* code. This will help you work faster and obtain better results.

4

Avoid Reinventing the Wheel

In the preceding chapters, you learned how to use *Less* to compile your CSS. *Less* helps you create reusable and maintainable CSS code. You have learned how to organize your files and the previous chapter also showed you the role of namespaces to make your code portable. *Less* helps you write efficient code to handle browser incompatibility. *Less* doesn't solve problems with browser incompatibility on its own but makes your solutions reusable, although the reusable mixins can still be complex for this reason. In this chapter, you will learn that you won't have to write all this complex code yourself. There are some libraries of prebuilt mixins out there which can help you work faster and create more stable code.

This chapter will cover the following topics:

- Background gradients
- Preventing unused code
- Testing your code
- The iconic fonts of prebuilt mixins
- Retina.js

Revisiting background gradients

Remember the CSS3 background gradient that was discussed in *Chapter 2, Using Variables and Mixins*? To show a better or the same gradient on different browsers, you have to use vendor-specific rules. Different sets of rules make your mixins more complex. In this case, more complex also means more difficult to maintain.

In practice, your mixins grow with outdated code or with code that is no longer supported on the one hand, while you have to update your mixins for newer browsers on the other. Of course, we can only hope that new browser versions support CSS3 specifications without any further changes to the code.

The **Can I use...** website (http://caniuse.com/) provides compatibility tables for HTML5, CSS3, and SVG support, and also for desktop and mobile browsers. It will show you that most of the current browsers have support for CSS gradients in their current version. At the time of writing this book, the Android browser for mobile still relies on the -webkit vendor rule, and Opera Mini doesn't support it at all.

If you drop the support for older browsers, your mixin can be reduced to the following code snippet:

```
.verticalgradient(@start-color: black; @end-color: white; @start-percent: 0%; @end-percent: 100%) {
    background-image: -webkit-linear-gradient(top, @start-color @start-percent, @end-color @end-percent);
    background-image: linear-gradient(to bottom, @start-color @start-percent, @end-color @end-percent);
    background-repeat: repeat-x;
}
```

The preceding code also drops support for IE8 and IE9. If you choose to support these browsers too, you have to add an additional IE-specific rule. The **Can I use...** website also shows you market shares of the most common browsers. In some cases, it can also be useful to only provide functional support for older browsers and not expect everything to look exactly the same on all browsers. For instance, a navigation structure without advanced animations can still help the user navigate through your site. People who use an older browser do not always expect the newest techniques. These techniques also do not always have added value. Older browsers mostly don't run on the newest hardware; on these browsers, support for features such as gradients will only slow down your website instead of adding any value.

Unused code

Even when using *Less* for long running and growing projects, it's almost impossible to not find some unused pieces of code in your code. Browser tools can help detect this unused code in your final CSS.

Chrome's developer tools

Google Chrome's developer tools have an option to find unused CSS. In Google Chrome, navigate to **Tools | Developers Tools**, select the **Audits** tab, and click on **Run**.

Now use this tool to test the demo code from the preceding chapters.

To start, open `http://localhost/index.html` in your browser and run the test. You will see the following screenshot:

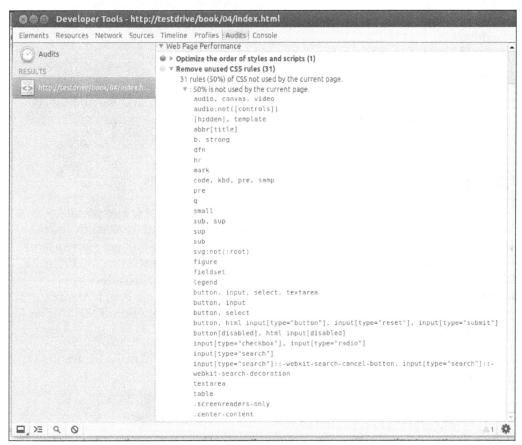

Unused code shown by Chrome's developer tools

The list of unused code starts with a long list of styles defined in `less/normalize.less`, as seen in *Chapter 1, Improve Web Development with Less*; these are the styles of the **CSS reset**.

In most projects, the same base of CSS code (the same file) is used for every page. For this reason, you cannot always guarantee that a page includes only the code that it really uses. Some of this code won't be used on every page but will have to be used on other or future pages. Web browsers are able to cache CSS files, for this reason it is better to use the same CSS file to style different pages from your website. Some pages will not use all the cached style rules which will be shown as unused code on that page. Cached code is loaded once and used on every page. The CSS reset seems useful for all pages, so you should not change or remove it.

As you can also see, `.centercontent` and `.screen-readeronly` are unused. Remember that classes are compiled into your CSS while mixins are not. Now, `.centercontent` and `.screen-readeronly` are defined as classes. Having a `.screen-readeronly` class seems useful, but `.centercontent` can be changed to a mixin.

Firebug CSS usage add-on

For Firefox, an add-on for Firebug is available. This helps you find the unused code. You can download this plugin at `https://addons.mozilla.org/en-US/firefox/addon/css-usage/`.

Testing your code

You don't have to write all the *Less* code yourself as it is reusable and portable. Mixins and snippets of *Less* code can be found on the Web and (re)used in your projects. Search for *Less* mixin background gradients and you will get many useful hits. Try to find code that offers support for browsers and meets your requirements. If you have any doubts about the browser support of a mixin, consider asking questions on Stackoverflow.com (`http://www.stackoverflow.com/`). Always show your code and what you have done; don't just ask for a solution. Also, other questions regarding *Less* can be asked on Stackoverflow.com.

Integration of code snippets or even complete namespaces will make the testing of your code more important.

Understanding TDD

Test-driven development (**TDD**) is a proven method for software development. In TDD, you write tests for every piece of code in your project. All tests should pass after changing your code when adding or improving functionalities or refactoring the code. All tests should run automatically. While automatically testing *Less* and CSS code, you need to manually look at the exact appearance of the pages in different browsers and devices, although other aspects such as correctness and performance can be tested automatically. You can, for instance, automatically test your code with tools such as **CSS Lint** (`http://ccslint.net/`). CSS Lint validates and tests your code, among other things, for performance, maintainability, and accessibility. These tools test the compiled CSS and not your *Less* code. The **Less Lint Grunt** plugin compiles your *Less* files, runs the generated CSS through CSS Lint, and outputs the offending *Less* line for any CSS Lint errors that are found. More information can be found by visiting `https://www.npmjs.org/package/grunt-lesslint`.

All about style guides

A **style guide** gives an oversight of your website's elements, such as buttons, navigation structures, headings, and fonts. It shows the elements in the right presentation and colors. Creating style guides for your project and website can help you test your *Less* code. Style guides will also help other developers and content publishers of your project.

You may be thinking now that style guides are indeed useful but also time consuming; for this reason, two tools will be discussed in the following sections. These tools generate your style guides automatically based on your *Less* (or compiled CSS) code. Both tools still require some additional code and effort, but it won't take too much of your time. Testing your code nearly always pays you back. Also, realize the big win here: you only have to test the effect of your styles. *Less* guarantees that your CSS is already valid, and the *Less* compiler handles it's optimization. As promised, it provides more time for your real design tasks.

Building a style guide with StyleDocco

StyleDocco generates documentation and style guide documents from your style sheets. StyleDocco works very well with *Less* files too. To create a style guide with StyleDocco, you will have to add comments to your *Less* files. The comments should explain what the style does and also contain HTML example code. The comments need to be written in **Markdown**. Markdown is a plain text format that can be easily converted into HTML. StackOverflow.com uses Markdown for posts and comments. You can use its help guide to learn more; you will find it by visiting `http://www.stackoverflow.com/editing-help/`.

StyleDocco can be installed with **npm** using the following command:

```
npm install -g styledocco
```

You have read about npm in *Chapter 1, Improving Web Development with Less*. After installing StyleDocco, you will have to add the Markdown comments to your *Less* files.

To see an example of a style guide generated with StyleDocco, open `less/nav.less` in your text editor and add the description in Markdown followed by the HTML test code, as shown in the following code snippet:

```
/* Construct a navigation structure.

    <ul class="nav">
        <li><a href="#">item 1</a></li>
        <li><a href="#">item 2</a></li>
```

```
            <li class="active"><a href="#">item 3</a></li>
      </ul>
  */
```

To build your style guide, navigate to your *Less* folder (`lessc`) in the terminal and run the following command:

```
styledocco -n "Less Web Development Essentials Styleguide"
--preprocessor "/usr/local/bin/lessc"  --verbose [file path]
```

In the preceding example, the name of the style guide is set with `-n`. Mostly, you don't have to set the `–preprocessor` option if your file path contains *Less* files only. To build a style guide for your *Less* files, the command should look as follows:

```
styledocco -n "Less Web Development Essentials Styleguide" less/*
```

The `styledocco` command generates a new folder named `docs/`. This folder contains an `index.html` file, which can be opened in your browser. The final result should look like the following screenshot:

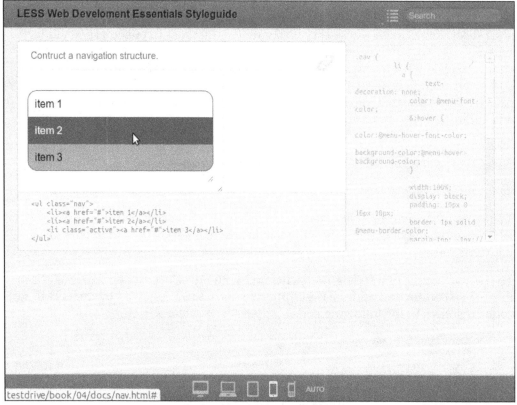

Example of a style guide built with StyleDocco

Testing your code with tdcss.js

The tdcss.js framework is another style guide tool that works well with *Less* and promotes the usage of test-driven development. The tdcss.js framework can be downloaded free of charge from GitHub at https://github.com/jakobloekke/ tdcss.js. Also, see http://jakobloekke.github.io/tdcss.js/ for further information. Unlike StyleDocco, using tdcss.js doesn't change your *Less* files. You generate your style guide with snippets of relevant source code from your project. You can use HTML-comment-style coding, for instance, <!-- : Navigation -->, to separate them. Snippets are copied and pasted to an HTML document which forms your style guide and includes styles from your *Less* code and tdcss.js. The head section of the HTML document of the example navigation will have the following structure:

```
<!-- Your Less code  -->
  <link rel="stylesheet/less" type="text/css" href="less/styles.less"
/>
  <script type="text/javascript">less = { env: 'development' };</
script>
  <script src="less.js" type="text/javascript"></script>

<!-- TDCSS -->
<link rel="stylesheet" href="tdcss/tdcss.css" type="text/css"
media="screen">
<script src="http://code.jquery.com/jquery-1.11.0.min.js"></script>
<script src="http://code.jquery.com/jquery-migrate-1.2.1.min.js"></
script>

<script type="text/javascript" src="tdcss/tdcss.js"></script>
<script type="text/javascript">
     $(function(){
         $("#tdcss").tdcss();
     })
</script>
```

The markup in the body is as follows:

```
<div id="tdcss">
    <!-- # Navigation -->
    <!-- & Style lists used for navigation. -->
    <!-- : Basic navigation -->
       <ul class="nav">
       <li><a href="#">item 1</a></li>
       <li><a href="#">item 2</a></li>
       <li class="active"><a href="#">item 3</a></li>
       </ul>
</div>
```

See the result of the preceding code by opening `http://localhost/tdcss.html` in your browser. The result should finally look like the following screenshot:

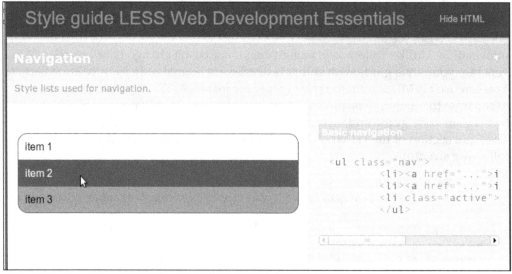

Example of a style guide built with tdcss.js

Prebuilt mixins

You already know about searching and finding mixins on the Web. However, using and reusing well-tested mixins will be a lot easier than that. Other developers have already built complete libraries and prebuilt mixins which you can use for your projects. These prebuilt mixins help you write *Less* code without having to think about vendor-specific rules that make CSS3 complex. You will be introduced to the five most used libraries in the following sections. These libraries are as follows:

- Less Elements (`http://lesselements.com`)
- Less Hat (`http://lesshat.madebysource.com/`)
- 3L (`http://mateuszkocz.github.io/3l/`)
- ClearLess (`http://clearleft.github.com/clearless/`)
- Preboot (`http://markdotto.com/bootstrap/`)

A more comprehensive list of mixin libraries can also be found at `http://lesscss.org/usage/#frameworks-using-less`.

Please understand that you don't have to choose; there is no restriction that you have to use only one of these libraries. All these libraries have pros and cons; you have to choose the libraries that best fit your project requirements.

Globally, all libraries offer you a *Less* file, which contains the mixins that you can import in your project. Although some libraries also have some settings, in all cases, `@import "{library-name}";` will be enough to make its mixins available for your project. *Less* has no restrictions on including more than one library, but doing this will give you problems with clashing mixin names. All mixins with the same name will be compiled into the CSS (if their parameters also match). For this reason, some libraries also have a prefixed version of these mixins.

Instead of the prefixed versions, using namespaces, as explained in *Chapter 3, Nested Rules, Operations, and Built-in Functions*, offers a more stable solution in most cases, as shown in the following code snippet:

```
// create a namespace for {library-name}
#{library-name}{@import "{library-name}";}
```

Make the mixins available using `#{library-name} > mixin()`.

Using single-line declarations for vendor-specific rules with Less Elements

Less Elements is perhaps the most compact library of the ones discussed in this chapter. Compact doesn't mean it is not useful. The focus of this library is on the consolidation of cross-browser prefixes into single, concise declarations.

Remember the vertical background gradient from the beginning of the chapter? You have seen that you will need at least three declarations, including vendor-specific rules, when you are supporting modern browsers.

With Less Elements, you can do the same with a single declaration of *Less* code with three parameters, as shown in the following code snippet:

```
element {
.gradient(#F5F5F5, #EEE, #FFF);
    }
```

The first parameter defines the fallback color used for browsers that don't support gradients. The gradient goes from bottom to top, where the second parameter sets the bottom color and the third parameter sets the top color.

The preceding *Less* code will finally compile into CSS as follows:

```
element {
background: #f5f5f5;
background: -webkit-gradient(linear, left bottom, left top, color-
stop(0, #eeeeee), color-stop(1, #ffffff));
```

```
    background: -ms-linear-gradient(bottom, #eeeeee, #ffffff);
    background: -moz-linear-gradient(center bottom, #eeeeee 0%, #ffffff
100%);
    background: -o-linear-gradient(#ffffff, #eeeeee);
    filter: progid:DXImageTransform.Microsoft.gradient(startColorstr='#f
fffff', endColorstr='#eeeeee', GradientType=0);
}
```

In its simplicity, Less Elements offers many useful mixins to build your project with **CSS3 techniques**. It provides single-line declarations for all CSS3 properties with vendor-specific rules and extends this with declarations for layout.

The .columns() mixin divides an element into columns, including a border and a gap between the columns. Variables for the .columns() mixin are in the order of column width, column count, column gap, column border color, column border style, and column border width.

This mixin can be applied on nonreplaced block-level elements (except table elements), table cells, and inline-block elements such as the body or div elements.

To divide a div element in to three columns with a width of 150 px, you can now write the following code in *Less*:

```
div.threecolumns {
  .columns(40px, 3, 20px, #EEE, solid, 1px);
}
```

The preceding code compiles into CSS and looks as shown in the following code snippet:

```
div.threecolumns {
  -moz-column-width: 150px;
  -moz-column-count: 3;
  -moz-column-gap: 20px;
  -moz-column-rule-color: #eeeeee;
  -moz-column-rule-style: solid;
  -moz-column-rule-width: 1px;
  -webkit-column-width: 150px;
  -webkit-column-count: 3;
  -webkit-column-gap: 20px;
  -webkit-column-rule-color: #eeeeee;
  -webkit-column-rule-style: solid;
  -webkit-column-rule-width: 1px;
  column-width: 150px;
  column-count: 3;
  column-gap: 20px;
```

```
    column-rule-color: #eeeeee;
    column-rule-style: solid;
    column-rule-width: 1px;
}
```

You can also test this by loading `http://localhost/columns.html` in your browser. Please also resize your browser window from small screens to full screen to see that these columns are responsive by default. The compiled `.div.threecolumns` class can be used with the following HTML code:

```
<div class="threecolumns" role="content">Vestibulum at dolor
aliquam, viverra ipsum et, faucibus nunc. Nulla hendrerit tellus
eu sapien molestie adipiscing. Cras ac tellus sed neque interdum
egestas sit amet vel diam. Aenean congue dolor et elit blandit
commodo. Pellentesque dapibus tellus eu augue ullamcorper dignissim.
Pellentesque pretium a dui a consequat. Curabitur eleifend lectus
vel viverra mollis. Sed egestas bibendum tortor mattis fermentum.
Suspendisse pellentesque facilisis blandit.</div>
```

The preceding code will result in the following screenshot:

Example of a multi-column layout built with the columns mixin of Less Elements

The `.columns()` mixin makes use of the **CSS Multi-column Layout Module**. More information about this module can be found at `http://www.w3.org/TR/css3-multicol/`. Unfortunately, the support for this module by most modern browsers is not good yet.

Less Elements does not provide any information about the browser support of the compiled CSS. You must have realized this when using Less Elements in your project. As mentioned earlier, you can check browser support on the `caniuse.com` website. To find out which browsers support this Multi-column Layout Module, you will have to visit `http://caniuse.com/multicolumn`. Always check the preceding module with the requirements of your project. Also, this example shows you why style guides can be very useful.

Less Hat – a comprehensive library of mixins

Unlike Less Elements, **Less Hat** is very comprehensive. At the time of writing this book, Less Hat contains 86 prebuilt mixins. Less Hat also has a strong relationship with CSS Hat. CSS Hat is a commercial licensed tool that converts Adobe Photoshop layers into CSS.

The Less Hat mixins offer the possibility of disabling some browser-specific prefixes. You should not use this unless you have extremely solid reasons for doing so. By default, Less Hat uses all the browser prefixes by setting the *Less* variables to true as shown in the following code:

```
@webkit: true;
@moz: true;
@opera: true;
@ms: true;
@w3c: true;
```

In the preceding code, @w3c refers to the nonprefixed rules that define the standard property names described by the **W3C specification**. Less Hat advertises itself as having mixins that create an unlimited number of shadows, gradients, and animations. **Box-shadow** is an example of this. With Less Hat, the box-shadow mixin can be written as .box-shadow(<offset-x> <offset-y> spread blur-radius color inset, …).

To try the preceding .box-shadow mixin, you could write it in *Less* with Less Hat as follows:

```
div {
  .box-shadow(30px 30px 5px green inset,-30px -30px 5px blue inset);
}
```

The preceding code compiles into the following code snippet:

```
div {
  -webkit-box-shadow: 30px 30px 5px #008000 inset, -30px -30px 5px
#0000ff inset;
  -moz-box-shadow: 30px 30px 5px #008000 inset, -30px -30px 5px
#0000ff inset;
  box-shadow: 30px 30px 5px #008000 inset, -30px -30px 5px #0000ff
inset;
}
```

To inspect this, open `http://localhost/boxshadow.html` in your browser and you will see the result of the `.box-shadow` mixin, as shown in the following screenshot:

Header

Vestibulum at dolor aliquam, viverra ipsum et, faucibus nunc. Nulla hendrerit tellus eu sapien molestie adipiscing. Cras ac tellus sed neque interdum egestas sit amet vel diam. Aenean congue dolor et elit blandit commodo. Pellentesque dapibus tellus eu augue ullamcorper dignissim. Pellentesque pretium a dui a consequat. Curabitur eleifend lectus vel viverra mollis. Sed egestas bibendum tortor mattis fermentum. Suspendisse pellentesque facilisis blandit.

Example of the effect of the box-shadow mixin of Less Hat

Indeed, the `.box-shadow()` mixin of Less Elements doesn't accept multiple shadows, but the mixin of 3L, discussed in the following section, works with multiple shadows separated with commas.

Using the 3L library of prebuilt mixins

3L (Lots of Love for Less) is another collection of prebuilt mixins. Besides the standard single-line declarations, 3L offers something extra. 3L provides mixins for CSS reset or normalization, as discussed earlier in *Chapter 1, Improving Web Development with Less*. You can call these mixins without placing them inside selector blocks as follows:

```
.normalize();

/* OR */
.reset();

/* OR */
.h5bp();
```

In the preceding `.h5bp()` reset, your CSS is based on **HTML5 Boilerplate**. HTML5 Boilerplate is a professional frontend template for building fast, robust, and adaptable web applications or sites. You will find more information on Boilerplate by visiting `http://html5boilerplate.com/`. 3L not only offers a mixin for HTML5 Boilerplate's reset, but also contains mixins for HTML5 Boilerplate's helper classes. These mixins contain a clearfix and mixins for hidden content for browsers or screen readers.

For instance, `.visuallyhidden()` can be used to hide the content for browsers but have this content available for screen readers.

SEO and HTML debugging

SEO (search engine optimization) plays an important role in modern web design. Correct and valid HTML5 is the requirement for SEO. Also, setting proper titles, using meta tags for keywords, and descriptions and alt attributes for images will help your website rank higher.

3L's `.seo-helper()` mixin will give you a quick insight into the missing elements and attributes of a web page.

To use this mixin—after importing 3L—you can write it in *Less* as follows:

```
html {
.seo-helper();
}
```

After using the `.seo-helper()` mixin, your HTML page will contain warnings about missing titles or meta tags and show a red border around images with a missing alt attribute, as shown in the following screenshot:

3L's helper class makes missing alt attributes visible

Also, visit `http://localhost/indexseo.html` to get more insight on how this class works. After this, you can judge for yourself whether this class is useful or not. Independent of your judgment, the `.seo-helper()` mixin shows you how *Less* can also be applied for functions other than a website's styles.

ClearLess – another library of prebuilt mixins

ClearLess also has a relationship with HTML5 Boilerplate. Just like 3L, ClearLess offers mixins for HTML5 Boilerplate and helper classes. Besides this, ClearLess also makes use of **Modernizr**. Modernizr is a JavaScript library that detects HTML5 and CSS3 features in the user's browser. Modernizr adds additional classes to the `html` element of your HTML for detected features. With Modernizr, your `html` element will look as shown in the following code snippet:

```
<html id="modernizrcom" class="js no-touch postmessage history
multiplebgs boxshadow opacity cssanimations csscolumns cssgradients
csstransforms csstransitions fontface localstorage sessionstorage
svg inlinesvg no-blobbuilder blob bloburls download formdata wf-
proximanova1proximanova2-n4-active wf-proximanova1proximanova2-
i4-active wf-proximanova1proximanova2-n7-active wf-
proximanova1proximanova2-i7-active wf-proximanovacondensed1proxima
novacondensed2-n6-active wf-athelas1athelas2-n4-active wf-active"
lang="en" dir="ltr">
```

This list of class names tells you whether a feature is available or not. So, the browser used to produce the preceding code offers support for box-shadow, opacity, and so on. With Modernizr, you will have conditional classes that can be used in your *Less* code. Also, ClearLess makes use of these classes.

Alongside the Modernizr mixins, ClearLess has mixins for icons and **CSS sprite images**.

CSS sprite images is a technique that dates back to at least seven years ago. A website's images are added to a single image, the sprite. If the browser requests an image, the sprite will be loaded as the background image. **SpriteMe** (http://spriteme.org/) can help you create sprites for your projects. CSS is used to show the requested image containing a part of the sprite. Loading one big sprite, which can be cached, instead of several small images will reduce the number of HTTP requests needed by the browser to show the page. The fewer the HTTP requests, the faster the page will load.

To demonstrate this, use the simple sprite of the *Less* image from the code bundle of this chapter (less-sprite.png) as shown in the following screenshot:

Example of a simple sprite image

To use the sprite image, you could write it in *Less* as follows:

```
#clearless {
@import "clearleft-clearless-63e2363/mixins/all.less";
@sprite-image: "../images/less-sprite.png";
@sprite-grid: 80px; //image height
}

.logo {
    #clearless > .sprite-sized(0,0,200px,80px);
    &:hover {
    #clearless > .sprite-sized(0,1,200px,80px);
    }
}
```

This code is also available in less/sprite.less. Please notice that the #clearless namespace got its own scope, so @sprite-grid and @sprite-grid should be defined inside the namespace. Variables are set by redeclaration.

The compiled CSS of the preceding code will look as follows:

```
.logo {
  background-image: url("../images/less-sprite.png");
  background-repeat: no-repeat;
  background-position: 0px 0px;
  width: 200px;
  height: 80px;
}
```

```
.logo:hover {
  background-image: url("../images/less-sprite.png");
  background-repeat: no-repeat;
  background-position: 0px -80px;
  width: 200px;
  height: 80px;
}
```

Load `http://localhost/index.html` to see the effect of the preceding code.

Finally, it should be mentioned that ClearLess defines some mixins to construct a grid. These mixins will be explained to you in the next section because they are adopted from **Preboot**.

Using Preboot's prebuilt mixins for your project

Preboot was originally written by Mark Otto (@mdo) and is a comprehensive and flexible collection of *Less* utilities. Preboot is the predecessor of Twitter's **Bootstrap**. Bootstrap is a frontend framework for developing responsive, mobile-first projects on the Web. You will learn more about Bootstrap in *Chapter 6*, *Bootstrap 3, WordPress, and Other Applications*. Bootstrap improved the original Preboot code. Finally, many of the *Less* variable and mixin improvements from Bootstrap were brought back in Preboot 2.

Preboot comes with mixins to build a grid system because of its relationship with Bootstrap. This grid system creates a row that contains 12 columns. Open `http://localhost/prebootgrid.html` from the downloaded code bundle in your browser to see an example with two rows. The first grid row contains three columns and the second row contains two columns. This grid is responsive by default; you can see this by making your browser window smaller using the example grid. If the screen width is less than 768 pixels, the columns in the grid will stack under each other instead of being horizontal. The following code example only shows the compiled CSS without the responsive classes.

With Preboot, you can write the following code in *Less*:

```
.col-a-half {
.make-column(6);
}
```

The preceding code compiles into CSS as follows (it is nonresponsive):

```css
.col-a-half {
  min-height: 1px;
  padding-left: 15px;
  padding-right: 15px;
  -webkit-box-sizing: border-box;
  -moz-box-sizing: border-box;
  box-sizing: border-box;
  float: left;
  width: 50%;
}
```

In *Chapter 5, Integrate Less in Your Own Projects,* you will find another example that makes use of Preboot's grid and discusses the responsive nature of it in more detail.

Preboot sets some variables to define the grid as shown in the following code snippet:

```less
// Grid
// Used with the grid mixins below
@grid-columns:          12;
@grid-column-padding:   15px; // Left and right inner padding
@grid-float-breakpoint: 768px;
```

Also, other values such as basic colors are predefined as follows:

```less
// Brand colors
@brand-primary:         #428bca;
@brand-success:         #5cb85c;
@brand-warning:         #f0ad4e;
@brand-danger:          #d9534f;
@brand-info:            #5bc0de;
```

In fact, Preboot is not a complete CSS framework; on the other hand, it's more than just a library of prebuilt mixins.

Integrating other techniques into your projects using Less

As well as prebuilt mixins, there are some other techniques that can be easily integrated in to your projects using *Less*.

Using iconic fonts

As the name suggests, iconic fonts are sets of icons defined as a font. Iconic fonts can replace image icons in your projects. The main reason for using iconic fonts instead of images and the reason they are discussed here is that iconic fonts, just like any normal font, can be fully manipulated with CSS. In your project, you can set the size, color, and shadows of the used iconic fonts with *Less*. The primary reason for using iconic fonts is to benefit the load time of your website; only one HTTP request is needed to load them all. Iconic fonts will look good on different resolutions and displays too.

In this book, iconic fonts were already used in *Chapter 3, Nested Rules, Operations, and Built-in Functions*. Font Awesome was loaded from CDN in these examples. Font Awesome also provides a bundle of *Less* files from GitHub at `https://github.com/FortAwesome/Font-Awesome/tree/master/less`. You can use these files to integrate Font Awesome in your project by performing the following steps:

1. Copy the `font-awesome/` directory into your project.

2. Open your project's `font-awesome/less/variables.less` file and edit the `@fa-font-path` variable to point to your font directory, `@fa-font-path: "../font";`.

3. Import the Font Awesome *Less* file in your main *Less* file, `@import "font-awesome-4.0.3/less/font-awesome.less";`.

After performing the preceding steps, you can use the following snippet of code in your HTML document:

```html
<ul class="fa-ul">
  <li><i class="fa-li fa fa-check-square"></i>List icons (like
these)</li>
  <li><i class="fa-li fa fa-check-square"></i>can be used</li>
  <li><i class="fa-li fa fa-spinner fa-spin"></i>to replace</li>
  <li><i class="fa-li fa fa-square"></i>default bullets in lists</li>
</ul>
```

The preceding code when opened in your web browser will result in the following screenshot:

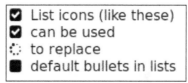

HTML list with Font Awesome items

You will find the *Less* code of the preceding HTML list in `less/font-awsome.less` of the downloadable files. Please inspect this file. You will see that you don't have to change Font Awesome's original files to set `@fa-font-path`. The `@fa-font-path` variable will be set by redeclaration and uses the last declaration wins rule as explained before in *Chapter 2, Using Variables and Mixins*.

You can find more examples of Font Awesome usage by visiting `http://fontawesome.io/examples/`.

Also, other iconic fonts such as Glyphicons for Bootstrap can be used with *Less* (see `https://github.com/twbs/bootstrap/blob/master/less/glyphicons.less`). However, in cases where you find iconic fonts without *Less* files, you now have enough knowledge to create the required *Less* code yourself.

Try to write the required *Less* code to integrate Meteocons (`http://www.alessioatzeni.com/meteocons/`) into your project as an exercise or perform the following steps:

1. Start by downloading the fonts from `http://www.alessioatzeni.com/meteocons/res/download/meteocons-font.zip`.

2. In this zip file, you will find four files: `meteocons-webfont.eot`, `meteocons-webfont.svg`, `meteocons-webfont.ttf`, and `meteocons-webfont.woff`. These are the different formats required to show the Meteocons in different browsers.

3. Copy these files to the `fonts/` folder of your project. You will also find `stylesheet.css` included with these font files. This file contains the `@fontface` styles for Meteocons. If you inspect the Font Awesome *Less* files, you will find the same kind of styles. The `@fontface` declaration is required to use the font in your project.

Now, you should remember the Less Hat prebuilt mixins. Less Hat has the fontface mixin, `.font-face(@fontname, @fontfile, @fontweight:normal, @fontstyle:normal)`.

Using this fontface mixin, you can add the following code to your *Less* code:

```
#lesshat {@import "lesshat/lesshat.less";}

@font-face {
#lesshat > .font-face("Meteocons", "../fonts/meteocons-webfont");
}

[data-icon]:before {
        font-family: 'Meteocons';
        content: attr(data-icon);
}
```

The preceding code will compile into CSS as follows:

```
@font-face {
  font-family: "Meteocons";
  src: url("../fonts/meteocons-webfont.eot");
  src: url("../fonts/meteocons-webfont.eot?#iefix") format("embedded-
opentype"), url("../fonts/meteocons-webfont.woff") format("woff"),
url("../fonts/meteocons-webfont.ttf") format("truetype"), url("../
fonts/meteocons-webfont.svg#Meteocons") format("svg");
  font-weight: normal;
  font-style: normal;
}
[data-icon]:before {
  font-family: 'Meteocons';
  content: attr(data-icon);
}
```

The preceding CSS code enables you to use the following HTML code:

```
<a href="" data-icon="A">Link</a>
```

The preceding code in HTML will look like the following screenshot:

Hyperlink with Meteocon

Earlier, you saw how Font Awesome icons can be added by class name. To add this functionality to the Meteocons, you will have to write some *Less* code. The following diagram shows the letter for each icon of this font:

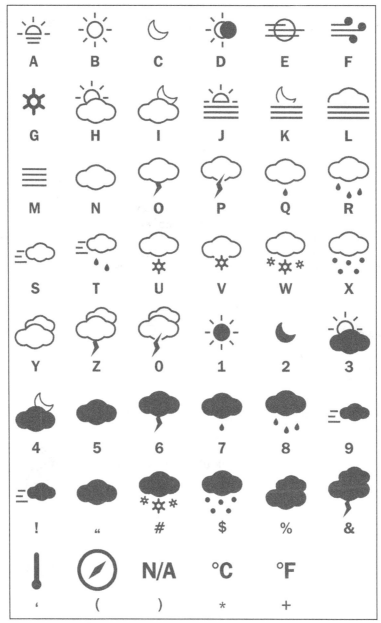

Meteocons font

Now, add a class declaration into your *Less* code for each icon as follows:

```
. meteocons-sun                  { &:before { content: "\2a"; } }
```

In the preceding example, `.meteocons-sun` is your class name, and `\2a` represents the hexadecimal value of a similar character. 2A hexadecimal is 42 decimal, and the * (asterisk) has an ASCII value of 42. Instead of a hexadecimal value, you can also use octal or decimal (for the first 128 printable characters). Sometimes, the `\u` of unicode is prepended, such as `\u002a` in the preceding code.

If you do add these class declarations, your list will look like the following code snippet:

```
.mc-light-sunrise:before {
  content: "\0041";
}
.mc-light-sunshine:before {
  content: "\0042";
}
.mc-light-moon:before {
  content: "\0043";
}
.mc-light-eclipse:before {
  content: "\0044";
}
and so on
```

Now, you have the basics for an iconic font, and you can extend your code. For instance, add the following code to set the size of the font:

```
.mc-2x { font-size: 2em; }
.mc-3x { font-size: 3em; }
.mc-4x { font-size: 4em; }
.mc-5x { font-size: 5em; }
```

In the download section of this chapter, you will find the complete *Less* code to use Meteocons the same way as Font Awesome in `less/meteocons`. As you see, most of Font Awesome's code can be reused. Please visit `http://localhost/indexmeteo.html` to find out how to use this code.

Retina.js

High-density devices have more pixels per inch or centimeter than normal displays. Apple introduced the term **Retina** for its double-density displays. If you zoom in on an image (or scale it up), it will become blurred. This is the problem web designers have to solve when designing for high-density devices. You may be wondering what this has to do with *Less*. CSS, in combination with media queries (you will learn more about media queries in *Chapter 5, Integrate Less in Your Own Projects*), can prevent your images from becoming blurred on high-density displays.

To understand what happens, you have to realize that CSS pixels are, in fact, device independent. CSS pixels are used to give physical dimensions to the elements in the browser. On normal screens, a CSS pixel matches a device pixel. High-density displays have more device pixels than a CSS pixel; in the case of Retina, they have four times the number of pixels. More and smaller pixels make it impossible to see the individual pixels with the human eye and should give a better user experience.

Retina displays an image of 300 CSS pixels width that requires 600 device pixels in order to keep the same physical size. Now you can prevent your images from blurring by using a bitmap with a higher resolution (CSS pixels) and scale it down with HTML or CSS.

On a normal display, your HTML will look as follows:

```
<img src="photo300x300.png" width="300px" height="300px">
```

While on a Retina display, you will show the same image with the following code snippet:

```
<img src="photo600x600.png" width="300px" height="300px">
```

Currently, there is a convention of adding @2x to the names of high-density images, such as example@2x.png.

You should now understand that you can use *Less* to write efficient code to give these different images the right CSS dimensions. The retina.js library (https://github.com/imulus/retinajs) helps you handle high-density images and displays; it combines JavaScript and *Less* to write your Retina code.

For normal images, you have to use the following code snippet:

```
<img src="/images/my_image.png" data-at2x="http://example.com/my_
image@2x.png" />
```

The preceding code will be handled by JavaScript, but you will have to use *Less* to set your background images. Here, background refers not only to the page background, but to every background set by CSS. Most modern designs use background images for layout; also, accessibility rules require decorative images set by CSS.

With `retina.js`, you can write the following code in *Less*:

```
.logo {
  .at2x('/images/my_image.png', 200px, 100px);
}
```

The preceding code will compile into CSS as follows:

```
.logo {
  background-image: url('/images/my_image.png');
}

@media all and (-webkit-min-device-pixel-ratio: 1.5) {
  .logo {
    background-image: url('/images/my_image@2x.png');
    background-size: 200px 100px;
  }
}
```

Also, the other libraries of prebuilt mixins mentioned earlier will have mixins to set Retina backgrounds.

Summary

In this chapter, you have learned how to keep your code clean and test it using style guides. You have learned how to use libraries with prebuilt mixins, which help you develop your *Less* code faster and more securely. Last but not least, you have learned how to use *Less* and iconic fonts and make your projects Retina-ready.

In the next chapter, you will learn how to integrate *Less* in your projects or start a project from scratch with *Less*. You will also learn how to organize your project files and reuse your old CSS code. And finally, you will build a responsive grid with media queries.

5
Integrate Less in Your Own Projects

Now it's time to integrate *Less* in your workflow and projects. In this chapter, you will learn to migrate your current projects or start a new project from scratch using *Less*. The techniques and tools to convert your CSS code to *Less* code will be discussed, and finally, you will learn to build and use responsive grids with *Less*.

This chapter will cover the following topics:

- Importing CSS into *Less*
- Migrating your projects to *Less*
- Starting a project from scratch
- Media queries and responsive design
- Using grids in your projects and designs

While working with *Less* and seeing how it addresses the problems of duplicate code and the inability to reuse your CSS, you should have wondered when to start using *Less* for your projects. Although this may be the most important question of this book, the answer is quite simple. You will have to start *now*! The problems with CSS can be some defects in your **design process**. There will never be an excuse to not solve the defects as soon as they are detected. If you don't start now, you probably never will, and you will end up spending too much time debugging your CSS code instead of working on your real design tasks.

Importing CSS into Less

As you already know now, valid CSS is also valid *Less* code. CSS code can be imported into *Less*. There are different ways to do this. After importing your CSS, you can run the result through the compiler. This offers you an easy way to start using *Less* in your current project.

Consider creating a **style guide** before starting to import your CSS code. Style guides help you test your code, as described in *Chapter 4, Avoid Reinventing the Wheel*. Also, remember that *Less* is a **CSS preprocessor**. This means you have to compile your *Less* code into CSS before taking it into production. Client-side compiling with `less.js` should only be used for test purposes! Only importing your CSS and compiling it back into CSS again makes no sense. After importing, you should start improving your code. Importing CSS also offers the opportunity to combine the pre-existing CSS with newly written *Less* code and allows you to do the conversion to *Less* iteratively and gradually.

Using the @import rule

Earlier, you saw that the `@import` rule in *Less* is used to import *Less* files into your project. This rule in *Less* is an extended version of the same rule in CSS.

In the examples in the preceding chapters, the `@import` rule was only used to import *Less* files. By default, each file is imported once. The complete syntax is as follows:

```
@import (keyword) "filename";
```

There are six keywords that can be used with this rule: `reference`, `inline`, `less`, `css`, `once`, and `multiple`. The `reference` keyword, for example, `@import (reference) "file.less"`, will make mixins and classes from `file.less` available, without compiling them into the resulting CSS.

This can easily be shown with an example. You can download all the example code of all the chapters of this book from the Packt website (`www.packtpub.com`). The example layout from the preceding chapters will be used here again. Please remember that the main file of this project, `styles.less`, imports the other project files. Now you can use this to reuse the navbar. Start by creating a new file and write the following code into it:

```
@import (reference) "styles";
.nav:extend(.nav all){};
```

These two lines will compile into the following code:

```
.nav {
  list-style: none outside none;
  padding: 0;
}
.nav li a {
  text-decoration: none;
  color: #000000;
  width: 100%;
  display: block;
  padding: 10px 0 10px 10px;
  border: 1px solid #004d00;
  margin-top: -1px;
}
.nav li a:hover {
  color: #ffffff;
  background-color: #004d00;
}
.nav li.active a {
  color: #000000;
  background-color: #00b300;
}
.nav li:first-child a {
  border-radius: 15px 15px 0 0;
}
.nav li:last-child a {
  border-radius: 0 0 15px 15px;
}
```

Please also notice that the preceding result contains the values as defined in `variables.less` from the original project.

The `inline` keyword is used to import code that is not compatible with *Less*. Although *Less* accepts standard CSS, comments and hacks won't get compiled sometimes. Use the `inline` keyword to import the CSS as it is into the output. As shown in the following code, the `inline` keyword differs quite a bit from the `css` keyword. The `less` keyword forces the imported code to be compiled. When using `@import (less) "styles.css"`, all code will be compiled as usual. In the meantime, the `css` keyword forces `@import` to act as a normal CSS import. The following code shows the difference between `inline` and `css`:

```
@import (css) "styles.css";
```

The output of the preceding code is as follows:

```
@import "styles.css";
```

Imported style sheets (with `@import`) in your compiled CSS code are declared before all the other rules. These style sheets can play a role in the **CSS precedence**, which is discussed in *Chapter 1, Improving Web Development with Less*. For this reason, you cannot apply advanced techniques such as namespacing, and you should import files that are not created using *Less* at the beginning.

CSS 2.1 user agents must ignore any `@import` rule that is present inside a block or after any nonignored statement, other than `@charset` or `@import` (http://www.w3.org/TR/CSS21/syndata.html#at-rules). If you import a file with the same name twice, only one will be compiled by default. The same will happen if you use the `once` keyword; on the other hand, if you use the `multiple` keyword, the file will be compiled in the output twice. The following code will give you an example of multiple output when using the `multiple` keyword:

If the `styles.less` file contains the following code:

```
p {
color: red;
}
```

And your *Less* code is as follows:

```
@import (multiple) "style";
@import (multiple) "style";
```

The preceding code will output the following CSS code:

```
p {
  color: red;
}
p {
  color: red;
}
```

Migrating your project

With the different import rules, you can start using Less in your project without having to change your code. After importing your CSS, you can start defining variables and using mixins step by step. Always check the output of your new code before you start using it for production.

Please remember that style guides can help you manage the migration of your project, and also don't forget that you have to compile your *Less* on the server side into CSS code before using it in production.

Organizing your files

Try to organize your files in the same way as in the preceding examples. Create separate files for your project's variables and mixins. If your project defined a style sheet in `project.css` earlier, your main *Less* file can look, for instance, like the following code:

```
@import "reset.less";
@import "variables.less";
@import "mixins.less";
@import (less) "project.css";
```

You will import your original `project.css` in the preceding code; alternatively, you can rename it as `project.less`. Also notice that you will finally compile a new CSS file, which will be used in your project. It's possible to use the same name for this file; make sure that you do not overwrite your original CSS file. Although your new CSS files should apply the same styles, these files are better organized and *Less* grantees they contain only valid CSS. The compiler will also compress the CSS file.

Converting CSS code to Less code

In the process of **migration**, you may prefer to not have to convert your code step by step. There are some tools available that can convert CSS code to *Less* code. These tools should be used with care. **Lessify** helps you organize your CSS code into *Less* code. Lessify puts rules for the same element or class together. You can use Lessify by visiting `http://leafo.net/lessphp/lessify/`.

Consider the following CSS code:

```
p {
  color: blue;
}
p  a {
  font-size:2em;
}
p a:hover {
  text-decoration: none;
}
```

After using Lessify, the preceding CSS code compiles into the following *Less* code:

```
p {
  color:blue;
  a {
    font-size:2em;
  }
  a:hover {
    text-decoration:none;
  }
}
```

You can find another tool called CSS2Less at `http://css2less.cc/`. Also, this tool only groups class and element rules. Lessify and Css2Less can help you a little when organizing your styles. Neither tool works with **media queries**.

From all that you have learned so far, it seems like a good practice to start your project by developing your *Less* code. So, start your project by building a style guide using *Less*.

Your `project.less` file can look like the following code:

```
@import "reset.less";
@import "variables.less";
@import "mixins.less";
```

Integrate the `project.less` file with the client side `less.js` compiler into your style guide. After this, start adding your design elements or alternatively, add comments in your code.

When you are done with your style guide, you can start building your final HTML code. If you have to build a responsive website, you should first determine which **screen sizes** you will need. For instance, mobile, tablet, and desktop can be a good choice.

To better understand how you can use *Less* in this stage of your process, the following two sections describe the role of **CSS media queries** in responsive design and teach you how to use **grids**.

Media queries and responsive design

Media queries is a CSS3 module and is a W3C candidate recommendation since June 2012. Media queries add the possibility of applying a style sheet to CSS only when a media query evaluates as true. A media query evaluates the device's type and device's features. The device's types are screen, speech, and print, among others, and the features are width, **device-width**, and resolution, among others.

Nowadays, the screen type and device's width play an important role in responsive web design. With the use of media queries, someone can restrict CSS rules to a specified screen width and thus change the representation of a website with varying screen resolutions.

A typical media query will look like the following line of code:

```
@media  { ... }
```

For instance, the following media query sets the font color to black when the viewport's width is larger than 767 pixels:

```
@media screen and (min-width: 768px) {
  color:black;
  //add other style rules here
}
```

In the preceding code, we can see that all the style rules between the accolades are only applied if the screen width is 768 pixels or larger. These style rules will follow the normal **cascading rules**.

Making your layout fluid

Until now, your layout has had a fixed width defined by `@basic-width`. A fluid design defines its widths as a percentage of the viewport or browser window.

To make your layout fluid, define `@basic-width: 900px;` in `less/responsive/project.less`. This set value will not define the width of your design any more but will only set the `max-width` variable after your changes.

After this, open `less/responsive/mixinsresponsive.less` in the `.center-content()` mixin and change `width:@basic-width;` to `max-width:@basic-width;`.

The header is now fluid, without any further changes. The footer columns are also based on `@basic-width`, so you will have to change them too.

The width of the footer columns is set by the following code:

```
width: ((@basic-width/3)-@footer-gutter);
```

Please change the width of the footer columns in `less/responsive/footer.less` using the following code:

```
width: ~"calc((1/3 * 100%) - @{footer-gutter})";
```

Browser support for the `calc()` function can be checked by visiting `http://caniuse.com/#feat=calc`. Also remember the note on `calc()` and the use of **string interpolation** from *Chapter 1, Improving Web Development with Less*. *Less* code is stateless, so these width calculations should be done by CSS in the browser. The browser has the real width in pixels the moment the CSS has been loaded, so the browser can calculate the column width in pixels and render it.

Finally, you will have to change `less/contentresponsive.less` and add the media queries to it. If the screen width is smaller than 500 pixels, the navigation and content should stack in your layout.

First, make `#content` and `#sidebar` fluid by setting their width to `width:  2 / 3 * 100%;` and `width:  1/ 3 * 100%;`, respectively. Now, the width is fluid and you can add the media queries. For `#content`, you should change the code into the following code:

```
width:  2 / 3 * 100%;
float:left;
@media (max-width:500px) {
  width:100%;
  float:none;
}
```

The preceding code sets the width of `#content` to `100%` if the screen width is less than 500 pixels. It also removes the float of the element. You should do the same for `#sidebar`.

After these changes for a screen width of 500 pixels, the navigation stacks below the content.

How to interchange the position of the navigation and content for a screen with a screen width less than 500 pixels can be seen at `http://localhost/indexresponsivechange.html`. You can accomplish this in two steps. First, interchange the content of `#content` and `#sidebar` inside your HTML document. Open `http://localhost/indexresponsivechange.html` and compare the source code with `http://localhost/indexresponsive.html`. After these changes, the sidebar will show on the left-hand side of the screen. To move the sidebar to the right, you should set its float to `right` instead of `left`, as shown in the following code:

```
//one third of @basic-width
#sidebar {
 width: 1 / 3 * 100%;
 float:right;
 @media (max-width:500px) {
  width:100%;
  float:none;
 }
}
```

On a small screen, the layout will now look like the following screenshot:

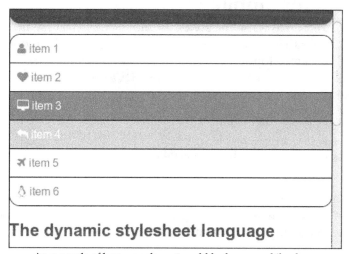

An example of how your layout could look on a mobile phone

Testing your layouts on a mobile phone

You will surely check your responsive layout on your mobile phone too. Make sure that you add the following additional line of code in the head of your HTML document:

```
<meta name="viewport" content="width=device-width, initial-
    scale=1.0">
```

The preceding code forces the mobile browser to load your website in a viewport that is equal to the screen width of your device. By default, mobile browsers load websites in a viewport that is larger than the screen size. Doing this lets nonmobile websites load as intended on a big screen. After loading the website, it's up to the user to scroll and zoom into the results. If your optimized mobile layout loads in a viewport with a width larger than 500 pixels, the media queries won't work, forcing the viewport to the device's screen dimensions, preventing the media query from not being applied. Note that this also means you will have to test this example with a mobile phone for which the screen is not wider than 500 pixels. You can also test your designs on websites such as http://www.responsinator.com/.

Coding first for mobile

Nowadays, it's common to write the styles for mobile devices first and then use media queries to alter them to fit bigger screens. Examples of the mobile-first principle of coding can be found in header.less and content.less from the files of your example layout. Also open less/responsive/footer.less and see how the media query adds the float:

```
@media (min-width:501px) {
    float: left;
    width: ((@basic-width/3)-@footer-gutter);
}
```

This example shows a **mobile first** way of coding. Elements stack by default and become horizontal when the screen size grows. Notice that older browsers such as Internet Explorer 8 do not support media queries and will always show you the stacked version.

Using grids in your designs and work flow

The preceding media query example did not use a grid. You may be wondering what a grid is and why you should use it. **Grid-based layouts** divide your design into a collection of equal-sized columns and rows. Content and graphical elements can be organized according to this layout. Grids help in creating a logical and formal structure for designs. It prevents inconsistencies between the original design and the final implementation in HTML as designers and developers work with the same grid.

Grids are also helpful in responsive design, because the grid's columns can easily be rearranged to fit different screen widths.

In the preliminary chapters of this book you already read about CSS modules that defined layout structures. Flex boxes and columns can be used to define CSS layouts and grids. Although these layouts are responsive by default or can easily be defined as responsive, they are not the common way to define your CSS layouts yet. As mentioned earlier, most modern browsers are not ready to support these modules. Luckily, there are alternative ways to define a grid with CSS.

The width of the columns of your grid can be defined as a percentage of the grid or a fixed width. Fluid grids define their widths as a percentage of the viewport. In fluid grids, the column widths vary with the screen width. Fluid layouts can rearrange the content to occupy the available screen width, so the user has to scroll less. On the other hand, designers have less control over the exact representation of the design. For this reason, the majority of responsive grids are a hybrid of fluid and fixed grids.

The role of CSS float in grids

The CSS `float` property is a position property in CSS; the float pushes the elements to the left (or right) side of the screen and allows other elements to wrap around it. For this reason, CSS `float` plays an important role in most **CSS grids**.

An example will help you understand how this works. You will create a grid with two columns. Start writing the *Less* code for a fixed grid. The example is as follows:

```
@grid-container-width: 940px;
@column-number: 2;

.container {
  width: @grid-container-width;
```

```
.row {
  .col {
            float: left;
            width: (@grid-container-width/@column-number);
  }
  .col2{
    width: 100%;
  }
  }
}
```

You can use the compiled CSS of the preceding code with the following HTML code:

```
<div class="container">
  <div class="row">
    <div class="col">Column 1</div>
    <div class="col">Column 2</div>
  </div>
  <div class="row">
    <div class="col2">Column 3</div>
  </div>
</div>
```

You can inspect the result of the preceding code by visiting `http://localhost/grid.html` from the downloadable example code of this book.

Now, you have an example of a fixed grid. This grid can be made fluid by changing the fixed width using the following *Less* code:

```
@grid-container-width: 100%;
```

In this grid, the `.container` class holds the grid. This container contains rows (defined) with the `.row` class. You have to define only two extra classes because this grid has two columns. The first class, `.col`, defines a single column and the second class, `.col2`, defines a double column.

Making your grid responsive

To make grids responsive, you have to define one or more break points. Break points define the screen widths at which a website responds to provide a suitable layout; below or above the break point the grid can provide a different layout. In the example grid, you can describe two situations. In the first situation, below the break point (for instance 768 px), the screens are small. On small screens (keep a mobile phone screen in mind), the columns of the grid should stack. Above the break point, for tablet and desktop screens, the grid should become horizontal and the columns of the grid rows will float next to each other.

In *Less*, you can write the first situation for small screens using the following code:

```less
.container {
  width: @grid-container-width;
  .row {
    .col, .col2 {
      width: 100%;
    }
  }
}
```

All columns get a width of 100% of the viewport and none of them float. Starting your code with the smallest screens first will generate a "mobile-first" grid. Mobile first designs start with a basic design for small screens (and mobile browsers, which, not always, have full CSS and JavaScript capabilities) and rearrange and add content when the screen size is bigger. You already saw that the grid became horizontal for larger screens. Other examples can be the navigation, which has got another representation, or an image slider, which is only visible for desktop users.

Have a go at making your grid responsive now by adding a media query and defining a break point in *Less*, as shown in the following code:

```less
@break-point: 768px;

.container {
  width: @grid-container-width;
  .row {
    .col, .col2 {
      width: 100%;
    }
    @media(min-width: @break-point) {
      .col {
        float: left;
        width: (@grid-container-width/@column-number);
      }
    }
  }
}
```

The preceding code compiled into CSS code will look like the following code:

```css
.container {
  width: 100%;
}
.container .row .col,
.container .row .col2 {
```

```
    width: 100%;
  }
  @media (min-width: 768px) {
    .container .row .col {
      float: left;
      width: 50%;
    }
  }
}
```

It's easy to see that now the `.row` classes only float on screens wider than 768 pixels. Width columns will stack if the screen size is less than 786 pixels.

The role of the clearfix

In the preceding example, columns became horizontal by applying `float:left` to them. The `clearfix()` mixin clears the float of an element after it has been rendered without additional markup, so it can be used for the `.row` classes of the grid. Using these clearfixes guarantees that your elements only float in their own row.

Using a more semantic strategy

In the previous section, you built a grid using `div` elements and CSS classes. Many CSS frameworks, such as **Twitter's Bootstrap** and **ZURB Foundation**, construct their grids this way. Critics of the approach claim that it breaks the semantic nature of HTML5. For this reason, they sometimes even compare it with the old-school way of defining layouts with HTML tables. HTML5 introduces semantic tags, which not only describe the structure but also the meaning of a document. For instance, the `header` tag is semantic; everyone knows what a header is and browsers know how to display them.

Using mixins instead of classes could help you make your grids more semantic.

An example of such a mixin is the following *Less* code:

```
.make-columns(@number) {
  width: 100%;
  @media(min-width: @break-point) {
    float: left;
    width: (@grid-container-width* ( @number / @grid-columns ));
  }
}
```

The preceding code can be compiled using the following *Less* code:

```
/* variables */
@grid-columns: 12;
@grid-container-width: 800px;
@break-point: 768px;

header,footer,nav{.make-columns(12);}
main{.make-columns(8);}
aside{.make-columns(4);}
```

The HTML for the preceding CSS code will look like the following code:

```
<header role="banner"></header>
<nav role="navigation"></nav>
<main role="main">
  <section></section>
</main>
<aside role="complementary"></aside>
<footer role="contentinfo"></footer>
```

Please note that in the preceding code, `@number` sets the total width to `@number` times the width of a column, and the total number of columns in the preceding grid will be fixed to 12.

Building your layouts with grid classes

The `.make-columns()` mixin can also be used to create your grid classes, as shown in the following code:

```
.make-grid-classes(@number) when (@number>0) {
  .make-grid-classes(@number - 1);
  .col-@{number} {
    .make-columns(@number);
  }
}
.make-grid-classes(12);
```

The preceding code will compile into the following CSS code:

```css
.col-1 {
  width: 100%;
}
@media (min-width: 768px) {
  .col-1 {
    float: left;
    width: 66.66666666666666px;
  }
}
.col-2 {
  width: 100%;
}
@media (min-width: 768px) {
  .col-2 {
    float: left;
    width: 133.33333333333331px;
  }
}
...
.col-12 {

  width: 100%;

}

@media (min-width: 768px) {

  .col-12 {

    float: left;

    width: 800px;

  }

}
```

In the preceding code, the mixins to build the grid classes are called recursively. Please recall *Chapter 3, Nested Rules, Operations, and Built-in Functions*, in which you have already seen how to use guards and recursion to construct a loop.

Building nested grids

If you set `@grid-container-width` to `100%` and make your grid fluid, the `.make-columns()` mixin can also be used to build nested grids.

Visit `http://localhost/nestedgrid.html` for an example of such a nested grid.

In HTML, you could write the following code to create a page with a header, content part, sidebar, and footer:

```
<div class="container">
<header role="banner">header</header>
<section id="content" role="content">
  <div class="content-column">Column 1</div>
  <div class="content-column">Column 2</div>
  <div class="content-column">Column 3</div>
</section>
<aside role="complementary">sidebar</aside>
<footer role="contentinfo">footer</footer>
</div>
```

The content part will be divided into three equal-sized columns. To archive the preceding code, you could write the following code in *Less*:

```
.make-columns(@number) {
  width: 100%;
  @media(min-width: @break-point) {
    float: left;
    width: (@grid-container-width* ( @number / @grid-columns ));
  }
}

/* variables */
@grid-columns: 12;
@grid-container-width: 100%;
@break-point: 768px;

header,footer{.make-columns(12);}
section#content {
  .make-columns(8);
  div.content-column {
    .make-columns(4);
  }
}
#sidebar{.make-columns(4);}
```

Here, the `.make-columns(4);` statement for `div.content-column` will create a width of `33.3%` (*4/12 * 100%*). The 33.3 percent will be calculated of the direct parent. The direct parent of `div.content-column` is `section#content` in this example. The `section#content` HTML element itself gets a width of 66.6 percent (*8/12 *100%*) of the viewport.

> Please note that if you should use the preceding grid in your project, you should separate your code into different files. If you create different files for your variables and mixins, your code will be clear and clean.

Alternative grids

In the preceding example, you have seen the grid defined with columns that become horizontal when the screen size increases. These grids use CSS float to align the columns next to each other. In some situations, mostly for older browsers, this may cause some problems in pixel calculation. This problem is sometimes described as the "subpixel rounding" problem. Although `box-sizing: border-box;` will fix related issues, as described in *Chapter 1, Improving Web Development with Less,* one can choose to use a different grid definition.

CSS isolation provides a solution. CSS isolation is not easy to understand. Susy (`http://susydocs.oddbird.net/`) describes it as follows:

> *Every float is positioned relative to its container, rather than the float before it. It's a bit of a hack, and removes content from the flow, so I don't recommend building your entire layout on isolated floats, but it can be very useful as a spot-check when rounding errors are really causing you a headache.*

CSS isolation is originally a part of Zen Grids (`http://zengrids.com/`). Zen Grid implementation has been written in SCSS/SASS. It will be relatively easy to rewrite this to *Less*; you could try this as an exercise. If you want to try this grid system, you can also download some example *Less* code from `https://github.com/bassjobsen/LESS-Zen-Grid`.

Building your project with a responsive grid

In the preceding examples, only the grid columns were defined. This should give you a good and realistic impression of how grids work and how to use them. A complete grid code also defines responsive containers and row classes. Most grids will also have so-called gutters between their columns. A gutter (mostly fixed) is a space that separates columns. This also means that a width spanning two columns include one gutter.

In *Chapter 4*, *Avoid Reinventing the Wheel*, you have learned to reuse *Less* and prebuilt mixins; you can do the same for grids. It won't be necessary to write the complete code yourself. Frameworks such as Twitter's Bootstrap, the Golden Grid System (http://goldengridsystem.com/), or Less Framework 4 (http://lessframework. com/) will provide you with all the *Less* code and mixins you need. Some of these frameworks will be discussed in further detail in *Chapter 6*, *Bootstrap3, WordPress, and Other Applications*.

The following examples will use Preboot's grid mixins to build your project's grid. Finally, you will rebuild the layout example you used earlier.

Using Preboot's grid system

Preboot's grid system enables you to build mobile-first grid layouts with a few variables and mixins. As you have seen earlier, you can use Preboot's mixins to create a semantic grid or define more general grid classes.

Preboot defines the grid's variables, which are shown as follows:

```
@grid-columns:         12;
@grid-column-padding:  15px;
@grid-float-breakpoint: 768px;
```

In the preceding code snippet, @grid-column-padding defines the width of the gutter, as mentioned earlier. The grid columns are coded with the mobile-first approach. This means that by default, they stack vertically and float horizontally when the viewport's width is equal to or is wider than @grid-float-breakpoint. Let's not forget, of course, that @grid-columns sets the number of grid columns.

Preboot doesn't provide a container that holds the rows of the grid. You could define this variable yourself to define a maximum width for your grid, as shown in the following code:

```
@grid-width: 960px;
```

There are three available mixins for each part of a standard grid system, which are as follows:

- `.make-row()`: This provides a wrapper for the columns to align their content via a negative margin and clear the floats
- `grid.make-column(n)`: This is used to generate n number of columns as a percentage of the available grid columns (set via a variable to 12 by default)
- `.make-column-offset(n)`: This pushes a column to the right by n columns via the margin

Now you can use preceding variables and mixins with Preboot to make a visible representation of the grid. To begin with, define some grid rows in HTML as follows:

```html
<div class="container">
<div class="row">
  <div class="col-12"></div>
</div>
<div class="row">
  <div class="col-11"></div><div class="col-1"></div>
</div>
<div class="row">
  <div class="col-10"></div><div class="col-2"></div>
</div>
<div class="row">
  <div class="col-9"></div><div class="col-3"></div>
</div>
<div class="row">
  <div class="col-6"></div><div class="col-6"></div>
</div>
<div class="row">
  <div class="col-1"></div><div class="col-1"></div><div
    class="col-1"></div><div class="col-1"></div><div class="col-
    1"></div><div class="col-1"></div><div class="col-
    1"></div><div class="col-1"></div><div class="col-
    1"></div><div class="col-1"></div><div class="col-
    1"></div><div class="col-1"></div>
</div>
</div>
```

The grid used here contains 12 columns and you can see the number of columns in each row should sum up to 12 too.

Now you can write the *Less* code for the preceding grid, which makes use of Preboot's mixins and variables. Again, you can split up your code into separated files to keep things clear.

The `project.less` file contains the following *Less* code which imports all required files into the project:

```
@import "../normalize.less";
@import "../basics.less";
#preboot { @import (reference) "preboot-master/less/preboot.less"; }
@import "variables.less";
@import "mixins.less";
@import "grid.less";
@import "styles.less";
```

The `variables.less` file contains the following *Less* code that defines the project's variables:

```
@grid-columns:          12;
@grid-column-padding:   30px;
@grid-float-breakpoint: 768px;
@grid-width: 1200px;
```

The `mixins.less` file contains the mixins for the project:

```
.make-grid-classes(@number) when (@number>0) {

  .make-grid-classes(@number - 1);
  .col-@{number} {
    #preboot > .make-column(@number);
  }
}
```

Note the usage of the `#preboot > .make-column(@number);` namespace here. The loop construct should now look familiar to you.

And the `grid.less` file contains the *Less* code, which defines the grid's classes:

```
.container {
max-width: @grid-width;
padding: 0 @grid-column-padding;
}
.row {
  #preboot > .make-row()
}
& { .make-grid-classes(12); }
```

The preceding code will create the CSS classes for your grid. Note that the `.container` class will be used to set the maximum width for the grid. It also sets a padding, which is needed to correct the gutter around the grid. Each row has a padding of half the size of `@grid-column-padding`. Between two rows, the `.containter` class makes the gutter equal to `@grid-column-padding`, but now, the left- and right-hand side of the grid only has a padding that is half the size of `@grid-column-padding`. The `.row` class corrects this by adding a negative margin of half the size of `@grid-column-padding`. Finally, the padding of the container prevents this negative margin from putting the grid off the screen.

Please also notice the ampersand in the `& { .make-grid-classes(12); }` statement. This ampersand (reference) guarantees that the inherited `.make-row` mixin will be visible when you need it. The namespaced mixin is not visible in the global scope. This problem may be fixed in later versions of *Less*.

And finally the `styles.less` file contains the *Less* code which defines the styles to make the grid columns visible:

```
.row [class^="col-"]{
  background-color: purple;
  height: 40px;
  border: 2px solid white;
}
```

The compiled CSS from `styles.less` will only be used to make the grid columns visible. As mentioned in *Chapter 1*, *Improving Web Development with Less*, `[class^="col-"]` is a **CSS selector** that selects your grid's columns which have a class starting with `col-`, your grid's columns. Each column gets a height (`height`), background color (`background-color`), and border (`border`). Also, here, the `box-sizing: border-box;` statement guarantees that the border width does not influence the width of the columns.

You can see the final result by visiting `http://localhost/prebootgridclasses.html` on your browser. The result will look like the following image:

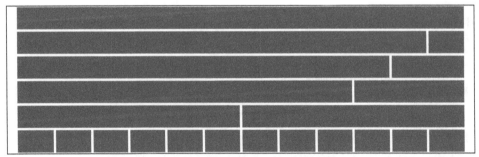

Representation of Preboot's grid with 12 columns

When you see the preceding representation of the grid, you may wonder where to find the gutters. As mentioned earlier, the gutter will be constructed with a padding of the columns. You can make this visible by adding some content in the columns. So, try adding the following code into your HTML file:

```
<div class="row">
  <div class="col-6"><p style="background-color:yellow;">make the
    gutter visible</p></div>
  <div class="col-6"><p style="background-color:yellow;">make the
    gutter visible</p></div>
</div>
```

After adding the preceding code into your HTML file, the result will look like the following image:

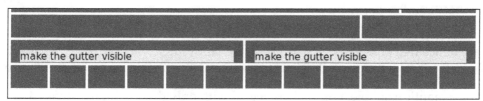

Preboot's grid with 12 columns; the content makes the gutters visible

In the preceding image you will see the gutters of the grid. Please also notice that the `.col-6` class only has gutters on each side, so the total content width of a `.col-6` will be 6 columns, including five gutters.

Using the grid mixins to build a semantic layout

In the preceding section, you used Preboot's grid mixins to build grid classes. In the final section of this chapter, you will use these mixins to build a semantic layout.

You can use the same example used earlier. Before you start, you should undo the changes made in the examples with media queries. You don't need these media queries here because the grid is responsive by default.

 You can watch the result by visiting `http://localhost/semanticgrid.html`, and you will find the Less files of this example in the `/less/semanticgrid/` folder.

In the current example layout, the container styles are applied to the body element. Nowadays, there seems to be no reason to add an extra `div` container (wrapper). All modern browsers handle the body as a normal block level element. If you prefer to add an extra wrapper for some reason, please do so. A plausible reason to do so would be, for instance, adding copyrights under your layout; of course, the body doesn't allow you to add something after it. In both cases, this container holds the grids' rows.

Open `/less/semanticgrid/project.less` and write the following *Less* code for the container mentioned into it:

```
body {
    max-width: @basic-width;
    padding: 0 @grid-column-padding;
    margin: 0 auto;
}
```

Please notice that `@basic-width` in `/less/semanticgrid/variables.less` is set to 900 pixels to make it clear that the grid is responsive with a break point at 768 pixels.

In this semantic example, you will use a grid with only three columns, defined in `/less/semanticgrid/variables.less`, using the following code:

```
/* grid */
@grid-columns:          3;
@grid-column-padding:   30px;
@grid-float-breakpoint: 768px;
```

In `/less/semanticgrid/project.less`, you can see that this example doesn't use a namespace for Preboot. The latest version of *Less*, when this book was written, doesn't support using namespace's variables in the global scope. In further releases, you can expect `#namespace > @variable` to work, but it doesn't work as of now. Using a namespace will make the setting of, for instance, `@grid-columns` inside the namespace from the global scope complex or impossible.

Now, open `/less/semanticgrid/header.less`. In this file, you can remove the old `.centercontent` class.

Use the `.make-row()` mixin of Preboot to make the `header` tag act like a row and use the `.make-column(3)` mixin call for `h1` inside this header. The `h1` element will have a width of three columns now.

Do the same for `/less/semanticgrid/content.less` but use `.make-column(2)` for the content and `.make-column(1)` for the sidebar here.

Again, you will see that in the mobile version, the navigation is under the content as explained earlier. You can fix this using the same trick you have seen earlier in the media queries example. In *Chapter 6, Bootstrap3, WordPress, and Other Applications*, you will learn other ways to solve problems like this. For now, reverse the sidebar and the content in your HTML code so that the sidebar is before the content. After this, you should give the sidebar a `float: right` call, as shown in the following code:

```
@media (min-width: @grid-float-breakpoint) {
  float:right;
}
```

Finally, you have to change the footer. Please use `.make-row()` again for the `footer` tag. The `div` elements inside the footer, which form the columns, will be styled with `.make-column(1)`. After doing this, you will see that the footer's columns are shown next to each other without any white space between them. Remember that the gutter of the grid is between the content of the columns and not between the columns itself.

To fix the problem mentioned earlier, apply `background-color`, `border-radius`, and `box-shadow` on the p element inside the `div` element, as shown in the following code:

```
div {
.make-column(1);
p {
  min-height: @footer-height;
  background-color: @footer-dark-color;
  //margin: @footer-gutter (@footer-gutter / 2);
  .border-radius(15px);
  .box-shadow(10px 10px 10px, 70%);
  padding: 10px;
  }
}
```

The preceding code will make the gutter visible, as seen earlier. The gutter of the grid adds some white space between the columns. There will also be a gutter on the left-hand side of the left column and on the right-hand side of the right column. This will make the total visible width of the footer columns smaller than the header. You can remove this gutter by setting the padding of div to 0 on these sides. Change the padding on the middle column to give the three columns the same width again. This can be done using the following code:

```
div {

  &:first-child {

    padding-left: 0;

  }

  &:nth-child(2) {

    padding-left: 15px;

    padding-right: 15px;

  }

  &:last-child {

    padding-right: 0;

  }

}
```

Visit http://localhost/semanticgrid.html to see the final result of the preceding code. Resize your browser window to see that it is indeed responsive.

Extending your grids

In the preceding examples, you used one grid with one break point. Below the break point, your rows simply stack. This seems to work in many cases, but sometimes, it will be useful to have a grid for small screens as well. Imagine that you build a photo gallery. On large screens, there will be four photos in a row. For smaller screens, the photos shouldn't stack but show up with two instead of four in a row.

Again, you can solve this situation using grid classes or mixins for a more semantic solution.

In both situations, you should also make your photos responsive. You can do this by adding styles for your images. Setting `max-width` to `100%` and `height` to `auto` does the trick in most cases. The `max-width` variable prevents images from being displayed wider than their original size and ensures that they get 100 percent of their parent's width in other situations. On small screens, these images will get 100 percent width of the viewport.

To make your images responsive by default, you can add the following code to your project's *Less* code:

```
img {
  display: block;
  height: auto;
  max-width: 100%;
}
```

If you prefer to make your image explicitly responsive by adding a class to each image in your source, you can you use the following *Less* code to make such a class:

```
.responsive-image {
  display: block;
  height: auto;
  max-width: 100%;
}
```

Adding grid classes for the small grid

When using grid classes, you have to change the original `.make-column` mixin from Preboot. This `.make-columns()` mixin sets the styles for a column and add a media query. The media query in the `.make-columns()` mixin lets the columns float horizontally for wider viewports. For the new small grid, you don't need a media query, because the columns shouldn't be stacked at all.

To accomplish this, you can split the mixin into two new mixins, as shown in the following code:

```
.make-columns(@columns) {
  // Prevent columns from collapsing when empty
  min-height: 1px;
  // Set inner padding as gutters instead of margin
  padding-left: @grid-column-padding;
  padding-right: @grid-column-padding;
```

```less
  // Proper box-model (padding doesn't add to width)
  .box-sizing(border-box);
}

.float-columns(@columns) {
  float: left;
  // Calculate width based on number of columns available
  width: percentage(@columns / @grid-columns);
}
```

After writing the preceding mixins, you should also create two mixins which do a loop to make your grid classes.

The first mixin should look like the following code:

```less
.make-grid-columns(@number) when (@number>0) {

  .make-grid-columns(@number - 1);

  .col-small-@{number},.col-large-@{number} {
    .make-columns(@number)
  }
}
```

The preceding mixins will be called from `grid.less` using the `.make-grid-columns(12);` statement. These mixins will be compiled into the following code:

```css
.col-small-1,
.col-large-1 {
  min-height: 1px;
  padding-left: 30px;
  padding-right: 30px;
  -webkit-box-sizing: border-box;
  -moz-box-sizing: border-box;
  box-sizing: border-box;
}
.col-small-2,
.col-large-2 {
  min-height: 1px;
  padding-left: 30px;
  padding-right: 30px;
  -webkit-box-sizing: border-box;
  -moz-box-sizing: border-box;
  box-sizing: border-box;
}
```

After doing this, you can easily see that the preceding code can be optimized to the following code:

```
div[class~="col"] {
  // Prevent columns from collapsing when empty
  min-height: 1px;
  // Set inner padding as gutters instead of margin
  padding-left: @grid-column-padding;
  padding-right: @grid-column-padding;
  // Proper box-model (padding doesn't add to width)
  .box-sizing(border-box);
}
```

The second mixin will look like the following code:

```
.float-grid-columns(@number; @grid-size: large;) when
  (@number>0) {
  .float-grid-columns(@number - 1,@grid-size);
  .col-@{grid-size}-@{number} {
    .float-columns(@number)
  }
}
```

The preceding mixins will be called from `grid.less` using the following code:

```
.float-grid-columns(12,small);
@media (min-width: @grid-float-breakpoint) {
  .float-grid-columns(12);
}
```

The preceding code will create two sets of grid classes. The large grid classes will only be applied when the media query is true. You will perhaps wonder why you can't create these grid classes in one single loop. This is because of the *last declaration wins* rule; you should define all your large grid classes after the small grid classes. If, for instance, `col-large-2` is defined before `col-small-3`, you can't use `<div class="col-small-3 col-large-2">` because `col-small-3` overrules the styles of `col-large-2`.

After creating your mixins as described earlier, you can write your HTML code as follows:

```
<div class="row">
  <div class="col-small-6 col-large-3"></div>
  <div class="col-small-6 col-large-3"></div>
  <div class="col-small-6 col-large-3"></div>
  <div class="col-small-6 col-large-3"></div>
</div>
```

The preceding code will show four columns on your screen. These columns are wider than 768 pixels. The code will also show two columns on smaller screens. You can see an example of this by visiting: `http://localhost/prebootgridclassesextend.html`.

Applying the small grid on your semantic code

If you have chosen the semantic way to build your grids, the following example will help you to add a small grid to the footer of the layout you built earlier. You can use the files from `/less/semanticgrid/content.less` again in this example.

The layout has a break point at 768 pixels. Below this break point, on a small screen, the footer should have three columns, and on big screens, the footer columns should stack.

You can reuse the Preboot mixins you used earlier in this chapter to build a responsive grid, to create the footer columns as described previously. First, split the mixin into two new mixins: one mixin for floating and one for styling the columns, as shown in the following code:

```
.less-make-column(@columns) {
  float: left;
  // Calculate width based on number of columns available
  width: percentage(@columns / @grid-columns);
}
.iscolumn()
{
  // Prevent columns from collapsing when empty
  min-height: 1px;
  // Set inner padding as gutters instead of margin
  padding-left: @grid-column-padding;
  padding-right: @grid-column-padding;
  // Proper box-model (padding doesn't add to width)
  .box-sizing(border-box);
}
```

After creating these mixins, you can use them together with media queries as follows:

```
footer {
  .make-row();
  div {
    .iscolumn();
    .less-make-column(1);
```

```
@media (min-width: @grid-float-breakpoint) {
  .less-make-column(3);
  }
 }
}
```

Summary

Unfortunately, you have arrived at the end of this chapter. Hopefully, you feel that you are already able to start your own project with *Less*. In this chapter, you learned how to use *Less* for your projects. You also learned how to use media queries and grids to build responsive websites. You are ready to start using *Less* in your projects now. Finally, you will have more time for your real design tasks. In the next chapter, you will be introduced to other projects and frameworks using *Less*. You will also learn how you can use these for your projects.

6
Bootstrap 3, WordPress, and Other Applications

After reading the preceding chapters, you should have learned enough to build your own projects with *Less*. You will write better CSS and achieve more than you did before in the same time. You are definitely ready for the last step now. In the last chapter of this book, you will learn how to use *Less* with other well-known frameworks, applications, and tools. You will read about the web developer's tools that are built with *Less* or have integrated *Less* in their workflow. These projects can be used, customized, and extended with *Less* and will help you build better projects with *Less*.

This chapter will cover the following topics:

- Bootstrap 3
- Semantic UI
- Building grids with *Less*
- WordPress and *Less*
- Alternative compilers to compile your *Less* code

Bootstrap 3

Bootstrap 3, formerly known as **Twitter's Bootstrap**, is a CSS and JavaScript framework for building application frontends. The three in Bootstrap 3 refers to the third version of this framework; wherever Bootstrap is written in this book, it refers to this third version. The third version of Bootstrap has important changes over the earlier versions of the framework. Bootstrap 3 is not compatible with the earlier versions.

Bootstrap 3 can be used to build great frontends. You can download the complete framework, including CSS and JavaScript, and start using it right away. Bootstrap also has a **grid**. The grid of Bootstrap is mobile-first by default and has 12 columns. In fact, Bootstrap defines four grids: the extra-small grid up to 768 pixels (mobile phones), the small grid between 768 and 992 pixels (tablets), the medium grid between 992 and 1200 pixels (desktop), and finally, the large grid of 1200 pixels and above for large desktops . In *Chapter 5, Integrate Less in Your Own Projects*, you build a grid with Preboot's mixins; Bootstrap's grid works in a similar way.

The grid, all other CSS components, and JavaScript plugins are described and well documented at `http://getbootstrap.com/`.

Bootstrap's default theme looks like the following screenshot:

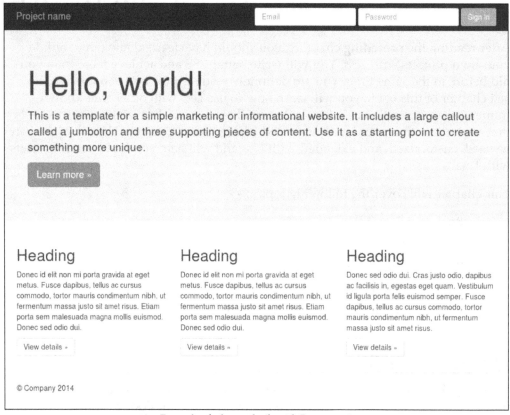

Example of a layout built with Bootstrap 3

The time when all Bootstrap websites looked quite similar is far behind us now. Bootstrap will give you all the freedom you need to create innovative designs.

There is much more to tell about Bootstrap, but for now, let's get back to *Less*.

Working with Bootstrap's Less files

All the CSS code of Bootstrap is written in *Less*. You can download Bootstrap's *Less* files and recompile your own version of the CSS. The *Less* files can be used to customize, extend, and reuse Bootstrap's code. In the following sections, you will learn how to do this.

To download the *Less* files, follow the links at `http://getbootstrap.com/` to Bootstrap's GitHub pages at `https://github.com/twbs/bootstrap`. On this page, choose **Download Zip** on the right-hand side column.

Building a Bootstrap project with Grunt

After downloading the files mentioned earlier, you can build a Bootstrap project with **Grunt**. Grunt is a JavaScript task runner; it can be used for the automation of your processes. Grunt helps you when performing repetitive tasks such as minifying, compiling, unit testing, and linting your code.

Grunt runs on **node.js** and uses **npm**, which you saw while installing the *Less* compiler. Node.js is a standalone JavaScript interpreter built on Google's V8 JavaScript runtime, as used in Chrome. Node.js can be used for easily building fast, scalable network applications.

When you unzip the files from the downloaded file, you will find `Gruntfile.js` and `package.json` among others. The `package.json` file contains the metadata for projects published as npm modules. The `Gruntfile.js` file is used to configure or define tasks and load Grunt plugins. The Bootstrap Grunt configuration is a great example to show you how to set up automation testing for projects containing HTML, *Less* (CSS), and JavaScript. This book can't handle all of this; more information about Grunt.js can be found in *Grunt.js Cookbook* available at `http://www.packtpub.com/grunt-js-cookbook/book`. The parts that are interesting for you as a *Less* developer are mentioned in the following sections.

In `package.json` file, you will find that Bootstrap compiles its *Less* files with `grunt-contrib-less`. At the time of writing this book, the `grunt-contrib-less` plugin compiles *Less* with less.js Version 1.7. In contrast to Recess (another JavaScript build tool previously used by Bootstrap), `grunt-contrib-less` also supports source maps.

Apart from `grunt-contrib-less`, Bootstrap also uses `grunt-contrib-csslint` to check the compiled CSS for syntax errors. The `grunt-contrib-csslint` plugin also helps improve browser compatibility, performance, maintainability, and accessibility. The plugin's rules are based on the principles of object-oriented CSS (http://www.slideshare.net/stubbornella/object-oriented-css). You can find more information by visiting https://github.com/stubbornella/csslint/wiki/Rules.

Bootstrap makes heavy use of *Less* variables, which can be set by the customizer.

Whoever has studied the source of `Gruntfile.js` may very well also find a reference to the `BsLessdocParser` Grunt task. This Grunt task is used to build Bootstrap's customizer dynamically based on the *Less* variables used by Bootstrap. Though the process of parsing *Less* variables to build, for instance, documentation will be very interesting, this task is not discussed here further. You will read about the customizer later in this chapter.

This section ends with the part of `Gruntfile.js` that does the *Less* compiling. The following code from `Gruntfile.js` should give you an impression of how this code will look:

```
less: {
  compileCore: {
    options: {
      strictMath: true,
      sourceMap: true,
      outputSourceFiles: true,
      sourceMapURL: '<%= pkg.name %>.css.map',
      sourceMapFilename: 'dist/css/<%= pkg.name %>.css.map'
    },
    files: {
      'dist/css/<%= pkg.name %>.css': 'less/bootstrap.less'
    }
  }
}
```

Last but not least, let's have a look at the basic steps to run Grunt from the command line and build Bootstrap. Grunt will be installed with npm. Npm checks Bootstrap's `package.json` file and automatically installs the necessary local dependencies listed there.

To build Bootstrap with Grunt, you will have to enter the following commands on the command line:

```
> npm install -g grunt-cli
> cd /path/to/extracted/files/bootstrap
```

After this, you can compile the CSS and JavaScript by running the following command:

```
> grunt dist
```

This will compile your files into the /dist directory. The > grunt test command will also run the built-in tests.

Compiling your Less files

Although you can build Bootstrap with Grunt, you don't have to use Grunt. You will find the *Less* files in a separate directory called /less inside the root /bootstrap directory. The main project file is bootstrap.less; other files will be explained in the next section. You can use bootstrap.less in the same way as you did in the earlier chapters.

You can include bootstrap.less together with less.js into your HTML for the purpose of testing as follows:

```
<link rel="bootstrap/less/bootstrap.less" type="text/css"
href="less/styles.less" />
<script type="text/javascript">less = { env: 'development' };</
script>
<script src="less.js" type="text/javascript"></script>
```

Of course, you can compile this file server side too as follows:

```
lessc bootstrap.less > bootstrap.css
```

Dive into Bootstrap's Less files

Now it's time to look at Bootstrap's *Less* files in more detail. The /less directory contains a long list of files. You will recognize some files by their names. You have seen files such as variables.less, mixins.less, and normalize.less earlier. Open bootstrap.less to see how the other files are organized. The comments inside bootstrap.less tell you that the *Less* files are organized by functionality as shown in the following code snippet:

```
// Core variables and mixins
// Reset
// Core CSS
// Components
```

Although Bootstrap is strongly CSS-based, some of the components don't work without the related JavaScript plugins. The navbar component is an example of this. Bootstrap's plugins require **jQuery**. You can't use the newest 2.x version of jQuery because this version doesn't have support for Internet Explorer 8.

To compile your own version of Bootstrap, you have to change the variables defined in `variables.less`. In the preceding chapters, you learned that you don't have to overwrite the original files and variables. When using the *last declaration wins* and *lazy loading* rules, it will be easy to redeclare some variables. Redeclaration of variables was discussed earlier in *Chapter 2, Using Variables and Mixins.*

Creating a custom button with Less

By default, Bootstrap defines seven different buttons, as shown in the following screenshot:

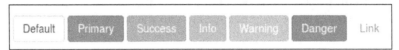

The seven different button styles of Bootstrap 3

Please take a look at the following HTML structure of Bootstrap's buttons before you start writing your *Less* code:

```
<!-- Standard button -->
<button type="button" class="btn btn-default">Default</button>
```

A button has two classes. Globally, the first `.btn` class only provides layout styles, and the second `.btn-default` class adds the colors. In this example, you will only change the colors, and the button's layout will be kept intact.

Open `buttons.less` in your text editor. In this file, you will find the following *Less* code for the different buttons:

```
// Alternate buttons
// --------------------------------------------------
.btn-default {
  .button-variant(@btn-default-color; @btn-default-bg; @btn-default-border);
}
```

The preceding code makes it clear that you can use the `.button-variant()` mixin to create your customized buttons. For instance, to define a custom button, you can use the following *Less* code:

```
// Customized colored button
// --------------------------------------------------
.btn-colored {
  .button-variant(blue;red;green);
}
```

In the preceding case, you want to extend Bootstrap with your customized button, add your code to a new file, and call this file `custom.less`. Appending `@import` `custom.less` to the list of components inside `bootstrap.less` will work well. The disadvantage of doing this will be that you will have to change `bootstrap.less` again when updating Bootstrap; so, alternatively, you could create a file such as `custombootstrap.less` which contains the following code:

```
@import "bootstrap.less";
@import "custom.less";
```

The previous step extends Bootstrap with a custom button; alternatively, you could also change the colors of the default button by redeclaring its variables. To do this, create a new file, `custombootstrap.less` again, and add the following code into it:

```
@import "bootstrap.less";
//== Buttons
//
//## For each of Bootstrap's buttons, define text, background and
border color.
@btn-default-color:            blue;
@btn-default-bg:                red;
@btn-default-border:           green;
```

In some situations, you will, for instance, need to use the button styles without everything else of Bootstrap. In these situations, you can use the `reference` keyword with the `@import` directive, as discussed earlier in *Chapter 5, Integrate Less in Your Own Projects*.

You can use the following *Less* code to create a Bootstrap button for your project:

```
@import (reference) "bootstrap.less";
.btn:extend(.btn){};
.btn-colored {
  .button-variant(blue;red;green);
}
```

You can see the result of the preceding code by visiting `http://localhost/index.html` in your browser.

Notice that depending on the version of less.js you use, you may find some unexpected classes in the compiled output. **Media queries** or extended classes sometimes break the referencing in older versions of less.js.

Customizing Bootstrap's navbar with Less

An important component of Bootstrap is the navigation bar. The navigation bar adds the main navigation to a website. It mostly contains a logo or brand name, a searchbox, and navigation links. In this book, navbar refers to the navigation bar. A typical Bootstrap navbar will look like the following screenshot:

Example of a Bootstrap navbar

Bootstrap's navbar is responsive by default. On small screen sizes, the preceding navbar will look like the following screenshot:

A collapsed and opened Bootstrap navbar

In addition to the CSS, Bootstrap's responsive navbar requires the collapse JavaScript plugin. This plugin should be included in your version of Bootstrap.

Now, try to change the colors of the default navbar as an example. To do this, you must first open `variables.less` to find out which variables color the navbar as follows:

```
//== Navbar
//
//##


// Basics of a navbar
@navbar-height:                    50px;
@navbar-margin-bottom:             @line-height-computed;
@navbar-border-radius:             @border-radius-base;
@navbar-padding-horizontal:        floor((@grid-gutter-width / 2));
@navbar-padding-vertical:          ((@navbar-height - @line-height-
computed) / 2);
@navbar-collapse-max-height:       340px;

@navbar-default-color:             #777;
@navbar-default-bg:                #f8f8f8;
@navbar-default-border:            darken(@navbar-default-bg, 6.5%);

// Navbar links
@navbar-default-link-color:                #777;
@navbar-default-link-hover-color:          #333;
@navbar-default-link-hover-bg:             transparent;
@navbar-default-link-active-color:         #555;
@navbar-default-link-active-bg:            darken(@navbar-default-bg,
6.5%);
@navbar-default-link-disabled-color:       #ccc;
@navbar-default-link-disabled-bg:          transparent;

// Navbar brand label
@navbar-default-brand-color:               @navbar-default-link-color;
@navbar-default-brand-hover-color:         darken(@navbar-default-
brand-color, 10%);
@navbar-default-brand-hover-bg:            transparent;

// Navbar toggle
@navbar-default-toggle-hover-bg:           #ddd;
@navbar-default-toggle-icon-bar-bg:        #888;
@navbar-default-toggle-border-color:       #ddd;
```

You have seen that it was easy to find these variables. The comments in the file are a handy guide to find them. You will also see that the meaningful and descriptive names for variables make sense, as learned in *Chapter 2, Using Variables and Mixins*. On the other hand, you may be wondering why there are so many variables only for the navbar. The navbar has many elements and different manifestations that need to be defined with variables. As mentioned earlier, Bootstrap's navbar is responsive by default; it collapses for smaller screens (or in fact, from the mobile-first point of view, it becomes horizontal for larger screen sizes). So, styles must be defined for both the collapsed and horizontal versions of the navbar. Colors for the navbar links and the collapsed menu toggle button are also set in the preceding code.

Just like Bootstrap's buttons, the Bootstrap navbar is also built with two classes, as shown in the following code snippet:

```
<nav class="navbar navbar-default" role="navigation"></nav>
```

In this case, the `.navbar` class provides layout styles, and the second `.navbar-default` class adds the colors and other variations. The `.navbar` class also has a third class that sets its type. There are four types of navbars: the default, fixed to top, fixed to bottom, and static top.

The navbar classes can be found in `navbar.less`. The navbar doesn't have a mixin to build the classes. The *Less* code provides classes for two alternate navbar styles: `.navbar-default` and `.navbar-inverse`.

As there are no mixins to use, redeclaration of some of the navbar's variables will be the best option to customize its look and feel. Optionally, you can copy the complete `.navbar-default` class and use it for customization. Bootstrap intends to use only one navbar per page, so additional style classes don't have added value.

For instance, now set the following:

```
@navbar-default-color:        red;
@navbar-default-bg:           blue;
@navbar-default-border:       yellow;
```

You can declare these variables into `customnavbar.less` and also add `@import "bootstrap.less";` to this file. Now, you can compile `customnavbar.less`.

You can see the result of the preceding code by visiting `http://localhost/customnavbar.html` in your browser.

Bootstrap classes and mixins

Skipping through the components, you will see that Bootstrap is a very complete framework. After the compilation of the framework, you have all the classes you need to build your responsive website. On the other hand, Bootstrap can also be used as a library. You have already seen how to use only the buttons.

In `utilities.less`, you can find the following code:

```
.clearfix {
  .clearfix();
}
```

The preceding code makes the `.clearfix` class available for direct usage in your HTML; on the other hand, you can still reuse the `.clearfix()` mixin. You can find Bootstrap's mixins in `mixins.less`. This strict separation of mixins and classes allows you to import `mixins.less` and apply these mixins into your own code under your own class name(s), without actually creating an output of these classes.

The preceding import of the `mixins.less` file will allow you to use Bootstrap's gradient mixins for your own projects, as shown in the following code snippet:

```
@import "bootstrap/mixins.less";
header {
 #gradient > .horizontal(red; blue);
}
```

The preceding code will compile into the following CSS code:

```
header {
    background-image: -webkit-linear-gradient(left, color-stop(#ff0000
0%), color-stop(#0000ff 100%));
    background-image: linear-gradient(to right, #ff0000 0%, #0000ff
100%);
    background-repeat: repeat-x;
    filter: progid:DXImageTransform.Microsoft.gradient(startColorstr='#f
fff0000', endColorstr='#ff0000ff', GradientType=1);
}
```

As you can see, the gradient mixins are namespaced. Please also visit `http://localhost/gradient.html` to see how the background gradient from the preceding example will look.

Theming Bootstrap with Less

As Bootstrap's styles are built with *Less*, it will be easy to theme your own version of Bootstrap. There are basically two ways to integrate your theme's *Less* code.

The first method compiles all code to a single CSS file. This method is recommended in most cases because loading requires only one HTTP request.

To use this method, import your theme file into `bootstrap.less` with the `@import` statement and recompile Bootstrap. Alternatively, create a new project file, for instance, `bootstraptheme.less`, which includes both, as shown in the following code snippet:

```
@import "bootstrap.less";
@import "theme.less";
```

This method overwrites Bootstrap's styles at the *Less* level, while the second method does the same at the CSS level. In this second method, the theme's *Less* code will be compiled in to separate CSS files, which will be loaded after Bootstrap's CSS.

Your HTML for client-side compiling will be as follows:

```
<link rel="stylesheet/less" type="text/css" href="less/bootstrap/
bootstrap.less" />
<link rel="stylesheet/less" type="text/css" href="less/yourtheme.
less" />
<script type="text/javascript">less = { env: 'development' };</
script>
<script src="less.js" type="text/javascript"></script>
```

Your HTML after server-side compiling will be as follows:

```
<link type="text/css"  rel="stylesheet" href="css/bootstrap.min.css"
/>
<link type="text/css"  rel="stylesheet" href="css/yourtheme.min.css"
/>
```

This second method requires an extra HTTP request when loading your page, but on the other hand, it offers the opportunity to load Bootstrap's core from CDN as follows:

```
<link type="text/css"  rel="stylesheet" href="//netdna.bootstrapcdn.
com/bootstrap/3.1.1/css/bootstrap.min.css" />
<link type="text/css" rel="stylesheet" href="css/yourtheme.min.css"
/>
```

The a11y theme for Bootstrap

A11y is a commonly used shorthand for (web) accessibility. Accessibility plays an important role in modern web designs; nevertheless, many websites pay less attention to it. The a11y theme for Bootstrap provides better accessibility with Bootstrap.

The a11y theme can be downloaded from `https://github.com/bassjobsen/ bootstrap-a11y-theme`. You only have to compile the *Less* file to use the theme. Also, in this case, you can choose between integrating the *Less* code into your *Less* code base or compiling a separate theme's CSS file. For more accessibility improvements of Bootstrap, also take a look at `https://github.com/paypal/ bootstrap-accessibility-plugin/`. Notice that this plugin doesn't provide any *Less* code, but only CSS.

Color schemes with 1pxdeep

1pxdeep helps you use **relative visual weight** and **color schemes** in your project. Based on a seed color, 1pxdeep's `scheme.less` file generates a color pallet with 16 colors. Each color is also defined in a variable. The variables, such as `@color1` or `@color4c`, can be used for the customization of your design. Every color variable also defines a class with the same name, so `@color1` in your *Less* code and `.color1` in your HTML refer to the same color in your color scheme.

After implementing 1pxdeep in your project, changing the branding or color scheme will be as simple as changing the seed color.

A typical `Less` project file using 1pxdeep and Bootstrap will look like the following code snippet:

```
@import "scheme.less"; // color scheme
@import "bootstrap.less"; // bootstrap
@import "1pxdeep.less"; // 1pxdeep theme
@import "style.less"; // your own styles
```

The preceding code redeclares Bootstrap's variables, such as `@brand-primary: hsl(hue(#428bca),@sat,@l-factor);`, and enables you to use 1pxdeep's variables such as `@color3` in the `style.less` file, as shown in the following code snippet:

```
header {
    background-color: @color3;
    h1 {
    color: @color3a;
    }
}
```

1pxdeep's CSS classes can also be used directly in your HTML code as follows:

```
<button class="btn btn-default color1">Color 1</button>
```

On 1pxdeep's website, you can test different seed colors to get an impression of how they look. Please visit `http://rriepe.github.io/1pxdeep/` and be surprised.

Using Bootstrap's customizer to build your own version

Whoever wants to start with a customized version of Bootstrap from scratch can also use Bootstrap's customizer. You will find the customizer by visiting `http://getbootstrap.com/customize/`. The customizer allows you to choose which *Less* files should be used. It will also be possible to set all Bootstrap's *Less* variables. The list can also be used as a reference for Bootstrap's variables when compiling a version yourself. Notice that the files that can be downloaded when using the customizer don't contain any *Less* files, so files from the Bootstrap customizer are not suitable for further customization with *Less*.

Semantic UI – another Less framework

Semantic can be used to build frontends too. Just like Bootstrap, it contains CSS components and modules. Components have been split up in to elements, collections, and views. Modules require not only CSS, but also JavaScript.

Semantic's name already makes clear that it pays attention to the semantics of HTML5. It is also tag-agnostic, which means you can use any HTML tags with UI elements.

In the following code, you will find a short HTML example that shows how Semantic is intended to be used:

```
<main class="ui three column grid">
  <aside class="column">1</aside>
  <section class="column">2</section>
  <section class="column">3</section>
</main>
```

Also, Semantic has been built with *Less*. The complete source, including the *Less* files, can be downloaded from `https://github.com/semantic-org/semantic-ui/`.

The way Semantic handles *Less* differs from Bootstrap and most of the examples you have seen earlier in this book. The Semantic source will also be built with Grunt, as described in the preceding Bootstrap sections. On the contrary, Semantic does not define variables and also doesn't define a master file that imports and connects the different *Less* files. The Semantic *Less* code is split up in to different modules in which most settings are hardcoded.

The different ways of handling *Less* by Semantic also means that when your projects use the framework in its entirety, you will always have to run the complete Grunt task after changing or extending the *Less* code. On the other hand, it will be very easy to use single Semantic components or modules in your projects. The components and modules do not depend on each other or global variables.

Please visit `http://localhost/semanticui.html` from the example files to see how this works. You will see that you can use the grid or buttons by including only the *Less* file. Also notice that if your buttons use icons (Semantic includes a complete port of Font Awesome designed by Dave Gandy for its standard icon set), you should also include the `icon.less` file.

Automatic prefixing of vendor-specific rules

When building Semantic with Grunt, the tasks first compile the *Less* files to single CSS files. After this task, the next task runs `grunt-autoprefixer`. The `grunt-autoprefixer` plugin parses *Less* or CSS and adds vendor-prefixed CSS properties using the **Can I Use...** database (`http://caniuse.com/`). The *Less* files in the `/build` directory are also prefixed this way. You can find more information on `grunt-autoprefixer` by visiting `https://github.com/nDmitry/grunt-autoprefixer`. The final tasks will bundle the CSS and JavaScript files in a single file and minify them.

Automatic prefixing will be very interesting for your future projects, because it enables you to write your *Less* code with single-line declarations only. Study Semantic's `Grunt.js` to find out how this works. For now, running task and automatic prefixing is out of the scope of this book. Notice that if you use single *Less* files from Semantic for your project, you will have to use the files from the `/build` directory instead of the `/source` directory. The *Less* files in the `/build` directory are prefixed while those in the `/source` directory are not.

Other frameworks to build your grid with Less

In the preceding section, you learned how to use Bootstrap and Semantic UI to build complete frontends. In practice for many projects, only a grid will be enough to start. You have seen that Semantic's grid can be compiled easily as a single component. Also, Bootstrap's grid can be compiled as a single component using the following code snippet:

```
// Core variables and mixins
@import "variables.less";
@import "mixins.less";
// Reset
@import "normalize.less";
@import "grid.less";
```

Alternatively, you could also use another grid system. Some of them are discussed in brief in the following sections.

Using the Golden Grid System to build your grids

The **Golden Grid System** (**GGS**) splits the screen into 18 even columns. The leftmost and rightmost columns are used as the outer margins of the grid; this leaves 16 columns for your design. More details about this grid system can be found at http://goldengridsystem.com/.

GGS comes with a *Less* file to compile the required CSS to build the grid.

 The **Frameless** grid system adapts column by column, not pixel by pixel.

The Frameless grid system, built by the same author who built GGS, is not fluid; the grid adds columns when a breakpoint has been reached. Notice that Bootstrap's grids work the same way. Frameless comes with a *Less* template that can be compiled to use the grid. This template contains a small CSS reset, some consistency fixes, as well as some basic customizable variables and functions for starting off a Frameless grid. More information about Frameless grids can be found at http://framelessgrid. com/. Frameless' documentation is sparse; however, you can find the source of Frameless' home page on GitHub. This will give you an impression of how to use it with *Less*.

The Semantic Grid System

The **Semantic Grid System** is very basic and effective. After setting the column and gutter widths, choose the number of columns and switch between pixels and percentages; you will have a layout without any `.grid_x` classes in your markup. The Semantic Grid System is also responsive. It also supports nesting and push and pull, which allows you to apply left and right indents to your columns.

Defining a fluid layout with *Less* will be as simple as compiling, as shown in the following code snippet:

```
@import 'grid.less';
@columns: 12;
@column-width: 60;
@gutter-width: 20;

@total-width: 100%; // Switch from pixels to percentages
article {
    .column(9);
}
section {
    .column(3);
}
```

Further information about the Semantic Grid System can be found at `http://semantic.gs/`.

WordPress and Less

Nowadays, WordPress is not only used for weblogs; it can also be used as a content management system to build a website.

The WordPress system, written in PHP, has been split up into the core system, plugins, and themes. Plugins add additional functionalities to the system and themes handle the look and feel of a website built with WordPress. Plugins work independent of each other. Plugins are also independent of the theme, and the theme mostly does not depend on plugins either. WordPress themes define the global CSS for a website, but every plugin can also add its own CSS code.

WordPress theme developers can use *Less* to compile the CSS of themes and plugins.

Using the Roots theme with Less

Roots is a WordPress starters theme. You can use Roots to build your own theme. Roots is based on HTML5 Boilerplate (http://html5boilerplate.com/) and Bootstrap. Please also visit the Roots theme website at http://roots.io/. Also, Roots can be completely built with Grunt. More information about how to use Grunt for WordPress development can be found at http://roots.io/using-grunt-for-wordpress-theme-development/.

After downloading Roots, the *Less* files can be found in the assets/less/ directory. These files include Bootstrap's *Less* files, as described earlier. The assets/less/app.less file imports the main Bootstrap *Less* file, bootstrap.less.

Now, you can edit app.less to customize your theme. You will have to rebuild Roots after your changes.

Roots' documents describe editing Bootstrap's variables.less file as the easiest way to customize a website built with Roots. More information can be found at http://roots.io/modifying-bootstrap-in-roots/.

JBST with a built-in Less compiler

JBST is also a WordPress starters theme. JBST is intended to be used with so-called child themes. More information about WordPress child themes can be found at https://codex.wordpress.org/Child_Themes.

After installing JBST, you will find a *Less* compiler under **Appearance** in your **Dashboard**, as shown in the following screenshot:

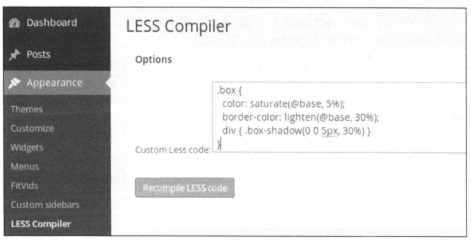

JBST's built-in Less Compiler in the WordPress Dashboard

The built-in *Less* compiler can be used to fully customize your website with *Less*. Bootstrap also forms the skeleton of JBST, and the default settings are gathered from the a11y bootstrap theme mentioned earlier.

JBST's *Less* compiler can be used in different ways.

First, the compiler accepts any custom written *Less* (and CSS) code. For instance, to change the color of the h1 elements, you should simply edit and recompile the code as follows:

```
h1 {color: red;}
```

Second, you can edit Bootstrap's variables and (re)use Bootstrap's mixins. So, to set the background color of the navbar and add a custom button, you can use the following code in the *Less* compiler:

```
@navbar-default-bg:              blue;
.btn-colored {
   .button-variant(blue;red;green);
}
```

Third, you can set JBST's built-in *Less* variables, for instance, as follows:

```
@footer_bg_color: black;
```

Fourth and last, JBST has its own set of mixins. To set a custom font, you can edit as follows:

```
.include-custom-font(@family: arial,@font-path, @path: @custom-font-
dir, @weight: normal, @style: normal);
```

In the preceding code, the parameters are used to set the font name (@family) and the path to the font files (@path/@font-path). The @weight and @style parameters set the font's properties. For more information, visit https://github.com/ bassjobsen/Boilerplate-JBST-Child-Theme.

More *Less* code can also be added in a special file (wpless2css/wpless2css.less or less/custom.less); these files will also give you the option to add, for instance, a library of prebuilt mixins, such as the ones discussed in *Chapter 4, Avoid Reinventing the Wheel*. After adding the library via this file, the mixins can also be used with the built-in compiler.

The Semantic UI WordPress theme

Semantic UI, as discussed earlier, offers its own WordPress plugin. The plugin can be found on GitHub at `https://github.com/ProjectCleverWeb/Semantic-UI-WordPress`. After installing and activating this theme, you can use your website directly with Semantic UI. With the default setting, your website will look like the following screenshot:

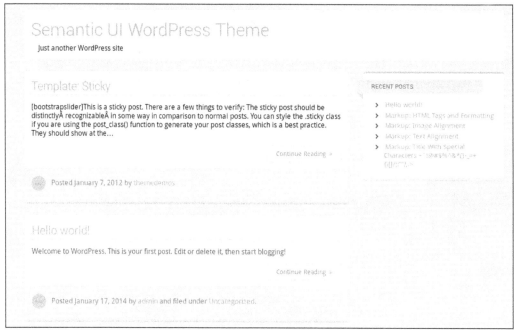

Website built with Semantic UI WordPress theme

WordPress plugins and Less

As discussed earlier, WordPress plugins have their own CSS. This CSS will add to the page as a normal style sheet as follows:

```
<link rel='stylesheet' id='plugin-name'  href='//domain/wp-content/
plugin-name/plugin-name.css?ver=2.1.2' type='text/css' media='all' />
```

Unless a plugin provides *Less* files for their CSS, it will not be easy to manage its styles with *Less*.

Theme WooCommerce with Less

WooCommerce is a popular e-commerce plugin for WordPress. With WooCommerce, you can build a web shop in a trice. You can theme your WooCommerce web shop with *Less*, as documented at `http://docs.woothemes.com/document/css-structure/`.

WooCommerce's *Less* file should be compiled into CSS and used as described earlier. To create a single CSS file for all your style sheets with *Less*, you can consider importing `woocommerce.less` into your project's master *Less* file and disable the default styling with `define('WOOCOMMERCE_USE_CSS', false);` in your theme's `functions.php` file.

The WP Less to CSS plugin

The **WP Less to CSS** plugin, which can be found by visiting `http://wordpress.org/plugins/wp-less-to-css/`, offers the possibility to style your WordPress website with *Less*. As seen earlier, you can enter your *Less* code with the built-in compiler of JBST. This code will be compiled into the website's CSS. This plugin compiles *Less* with the PHP Less compiler, `Less.php`.

Alternative compilers for compiling your Less code

With the growing popularity of *Less*, the *Less* compiler has been ported to other languages as well. These ports can be used to compile *Less* with native language calls. Please keep in mind that these ports will usually lag the official JavaScript implementation, so you may find they are missing recent *Less* features. You may also realize, as mentioned earlier in *Chapter 3*, *Nested Rules, Operations, and Built-in Functions*, that these compilers are not able to compile native JavaScript expressions within backticks.

The Less.php compiler

This PHP port of the official *Less* processor can be download at `http://lessphp.gpeasy.com/`. You have seen an example of its usage already; the WP Less to CSS plugin has been built with it. `Less.php` also implements caching for faster compiling.

Although `Less.php` offers the possibility of creating CSS dynamically, you still should precompile your CSS for production in most cases. WordPress is also written in PHP, so in the case of the WordPress plugin, *Less* can be compiled without using system calls.

In the following code, you will find a short example that will show you how to compile, customize, and use Bootstrap on a website written in PHP:

```php
<?php
require 'less.php/Cache.php';
Less_Cache::$cache_dir = '/var/www/mysite/writable_folder';
$files = array();
$files['/var/www/mysite/bootstrap/bootstrap.less'] = '/mysite/
bootstrap/';
$files['/var/www/mysite/custom/my.less'] = '/mysite/custom/';
$css_file_name = Less_Cache::Get( $files );
echo '<link rel="stylesheet" type="text/css" href="/mysite/writable_
folder/'.$css_file_name.'">';
```

The **lessphp** compiler available at `http://leafo.net/lessphp/` is an alternative PHP Less compiler.

The .less compiler for .NET apps

The `.less` compiler is a complete port of the JavaScript *Less* library for the **.NET platform**. If you want to statically compile your files, you can use the included `dotless.Compiler.exe` compiler. You can use `.less` for your web page by adding a new HTTP handler to your `Web.Config` file as follows:

```
<add type="dotless.Core.LessCssHttpHandler,dotless.Core"
validate="false" path="*.Less" verb="*" />
```

List of tools to develop Less

On the *Less* website (`http://lesscss.org/usage/`), you will find many other libraries, tools, and frameworks to develop *Less*.

Summary

In this chapter, you learned how to use *Less* with Bootstrap and Semantic UI and also got introduced to other grids and frameworks built with *Less*. You have seen how to use *Less* with WordPress, and finally, you saw how to use alternative compilers for your project.

This is also the last chapter of this book. In this book, you learned how to use *Less* for your projects. You saw how variables, mixins, and built-in functions can help you reuse your code. With *Less*, you can nest your style rules, which make your code more intuitive and readable. After reading this book, you know you don't have to write all the code yourself, but you can use prebuilt mixins written by others. Finally, you obtained knowledge on how to start projects from scratch with *Less* and integrate *Less* with WordPress, Bootstrap, and other tools. Now, you are really ready to start developing *Less*. Congratulations! You have enabled yourself to work better and faster using *Less* for your projects and will save more time for your real design tasks.

Index

T

tdcss.js framework
  about 99
  code, testing with 99, 100
Test driven development (TDD) 96
tools, for Less development
  URL 172
transformations
  about 28
  rotating 28
  scaling 28
  translating 28
transitions
  about 27
  example 28
transition-timing-function property 28
Twitter's Bootstrap. *See* **Bootstrap**
type functions
  about 89
  iscolor() 89
  isem() 89
  iskeyword() 89
  isnumber() 89
  ispercentage() 89
  ispixel() 89
  isstring() 89
  isunit() 89
  isurl() 89

U

unlocking 61
unused code, background gradients
  about 94
  Chrome's developer tools 94, 95
  Firebug CSS usage add-on 96

V

values
  escaping 49, 50

variables
  about 39, 41, 73
  files, organizing 42, 43
  hyphenated names 44
  last declaration, winning 46
  naming 43, 44
  organizing 45, 46
  semantic naming 44
  using 44, 45
variables.less file 139
vendor-specific rules, CSS 21
version
  building, customizer used 164

W

W3C specifications 11, 104
watch function
  about 17
  used, for automatic reloading 17
Web Essentials 36
WinLess 36
WooCommerce
  about 171
  with Less 171
WordPress
  about 167
  and Less 167
WordPress plugins
  and Less 170
WP Less to CSS plugin 171

Y

YUI CSS Compressor 36

Z

Zen Grids
  URL 136
ZURB Foundation 132

Thank you for buying
Less Web Development Essentials

About Packt Publishing

Packt, pronounced 'packed', published its first book "*Mastering phpMyAdmin for Effective MySQL Management*" in April 2004 and subsequently continued to specialize in publishing highly focused books on specific technologies and solutions.

Our books and publications share the experiences of your fellow IT professionals in adapting and customizing today's systems, applications, and frameworks. Our solution based books give you the knowledge and power to customize the software and technologies you're using to get the job done. Packt books are more specific and less general than the IT books you have seen in the past. Our unique business model allows us to bring you more focused information, giving you more of what you need to know, and less of what you don't.

Packt is a modern, yet unique publishing company, which focuses on producing quality, cutting-edge books for communities of developers, administrators, and newbies alike. For more information, please visit our website: www.packtpub.com.

About Packt Open Source

In 2010, Packt launched two new brands, Packt Open Source and Packt Enterprise, in order to continue its focus on specialization. This book is part of the Packt Open Source brand, home to books published on software built around Open Source licenses, and offering information to anybody from advanced developers to budding web designers. The Open Source brand also runs Packt's Open Source Royalty Scheme, by which Packt gives a royalty to each Open Source project about whose software a book is sold.

Writing for Packt

We welcome all inquiries from people who are interested in authoring. Book proposals should be sent to author@packtpub.com. If your book idea is still at an early stage and you would like to discuss it first before writing a formal book proposal, contact us; one of our commissioning editors will get in touch with you.

We're not just looking for published authors; if you have strong technical skills but no writing experience, our experienced editors can help you develop a writing career, or simply get some additional reward for your expertise.

Spring Web Flow 2 Web Development

ISBN: 978-1-84719-542-5   Paperback: 200 pages

Master Spring's well-designed web frameworks to develop powerful web applications

1. Design, develop, and test your web applications using the Spring Web Flow 2 framework.

2. Enhance your web applications with progressive AJAX, Spring security integration, and Spring Faces.

3. Stay up-to-date with the latest version of Spring Web Flow.

4. Walk through the creation of a bug tracker web application with clear explanations.

Instant LESS CSS Preprocessor How-to

ISBN: 978-1-78216-376-3   Paperback: 80 pages

Practical, hands-on recipes to write more efficient CSS, with the help of the LESS CSS Preprocessor library

1. Learn something new in an Instant! A short, fast, focused guide delivering immediate results.

2. Use mixins, functions, and variables to dynamically auto-generate styles, based on minimal existing values.

3. Use the power of LESS to produce style sheets dynamically, or incorporate precompiled versions into your code.

Please check **www.PacktPub.com** for information on our titles

Web Development with Jade

ISBN: 978-1-78328-635-5   Paperback: 80 pages

Utilize the advanced features of Jade to create dynamic web pages and significantly decrease development time

1. Make your templates clean, beautiful, and reusable.

2. Use Jade best practices right from the start.

3. Successfully automate redundant markup.

Node Web Development
Second Edition

ISBN: 978-1-78216-330-5   Paperback: 248 pages

A practical introduction to Node.js, an exciting server-side JavaScript web development stack

1. Learn about server-side JavaScript with Node.js and Node modules.

2. Website development both with and without the Connect/Express web application framework.

3. Developing both HTTP server and client applications.

Please check **www.PacktPub.com** for information on our titles